figureskating
now

figureskating
now

Olympic and
World Stars

Gérard Châtaigneau & Steve Milton

FIREFLY BOOKS

A FIREFLY BOOK

Published by Firefly Books Ltd. 2001

First Printing 2001

National Library of Canada Cataloguing in Publication Data

Milton, Steve
   Figure skating now : Olympic and world stars

ISBN 1-55297-527-4

1. Skaters—Biography. 2. Skating. I. Chataigneau, Gerard II. Title.
GV850.A2M54 2001   796.91'2'0922   C2001-901768-5

Publisher Cataloging-in-Publication Data

Milton, Steve.
   Figure skating now : Olympic and world stars /
Steve Milton ; photography by Gérard Châtaigneau. –1st ed.
[128] p. : col. photos. ; cm.

Summary: Biographies and photographs of contemporary figure skating champions.
ISBN 1-55297-527-4 (pbk.)

1. Skaters -- Biography. 2. Skating. I. Châtaigneau, Gérard. I. Title.
796.912 / 0922   21   2002   CIP   GV850.A2.M55

Published in Canada in 2001 by
Firefly Books Ltd.
3680 Victoria Park Avenue
Willowdale, Ontario, Canada M2H 3K1

Published in the United States in 2001 by
Firefly Books (U.S.) Inc.
P.O. Box 1338, Ellicott Station
Buffalo, New York, USA 14205

Design by Interrobang Graphic Design Inc.
Printed and bound in Canada by Friesens, Altona, Manitoba

The Publisher acknowledges the financial support of the Government of Canada through the Book Publishing Industry Development Program for its publishing activities.

CONTENTS

ACKNOWLEDGMENTS

To all the skaters, for providing such great inspiration over so many years.

To Firefly and the entire production team, including Kirsten for editing,
Christine for design, Michael for looking after everything and
Steve for delivering such good writing in so little time!

—Gérard Châtaigneau

Jessica and Toby, the perpetual muses.
Michelle who inspires everything.
June Burnside (ground zero) and:
Debbi Wilkes, Lois Elfman, Phil Hersh,
John Power, Mark Lund, Joyce Minten,
Paul Peret, Roland Zorn, Bev Smith, Shep Goldberg,
Marge Reynolds, Lori Nichol, Lorraine Quartaro.
And to Gérard, for his spectacular eye.

—Steve Milton

INTRODUCTION

A perfect moment forever frozen in time: that is the power of still photography, the power to explore a most extraordinary realm that exists at 1/500 of a second or beyond! In these tiny fractions of time, the camera can capture a hidden world, and what beauty is revealed when it is the world of figure skating!

The joy, the excitement, the power, the intensity, the greatness, the sheer beauty, it's all there, with an exceptional sophistication that, I believe, is unique to figure skating. This sport is a feast for the eye. It is also rich in emotions and expressions. The feelings and personalities of the skaters are center stage; they are an important part of performances that will captivate you and move you in ways you could never have imagined.

From Calgary to Nagano and just about all the World competitions in between (or after), I have seen a lot and, thankfully, I have been able to capture a fair amount on film.

A typical day of figure skating photography begins early during competitions. In 1995, at Worlds in Birmingham, I went to dance practice at 5 AM! That was the only way I could move unhindered and get the angles I was looking for. Would you believe that this early all the skaters were dressed up and the women were in perfect make up? No detail was left to chance, a perfect practice for the ultimate moment to come later that day, the ice dance final.

Discipline and dedication go hand in hand in figure skating. When you see a performance at a world championship, you can be sure there is a life of training and development behind it. Most competitors have started to skate at a very young age. They train each day on ice for six or seven hours; they attend off-ice sessions in ballet, ballroom dancing—indeed, they spend far more time training than the average person spends working a regular job. So, when you see a competitive program on Worlds' ice, it represents a phenomenal amount of effort, not just that all-important talent.

Over the last 10 years the quality of competition has climbed steadily. Skating now is at a level never seen before! Look at the top five in each discipline and you will see that they are all capable of gold medal performances. Then look at the top ten; again you will be amazed at how capable they all are and how close they can come to the podium!

One discipline that has evolved perhaps more than the others is ice dancing. Superb renditions, great speed and incredible complexity are common to all top teams. Creativity is always one of the main ingredients in dance, but now all teams have to confront required elements that give their technical ability a tough test. But you do not need to be an expert to enjoy the performances. Instantly you will know what is great and you will enjoy it to a degree beyond words that only the soul can appreciate.

Images have always been so important for me that I never really quite took the time to read much, until now.... I have known Steve Milton for some time and we would always see each other at competitions in some faraway places. Its funny that here we are, two Canadians, almost neighbors, but the only time we would speak to each other is in airports or press halls in Switzerland, Japan or some other country! Steve is fabulous at capturing the story behind the pictures; I hope that, together, we have made a book that will speak to all figure skating fans, wherever they may be.

—*Gérard Châtaigneau*

THE MEN

Evgeny Plushenko

Alexei Yagudin

Todd Eldredge

Elvis Stojko

Takeshi Honda

Timothy Goebel

Michael Weiss

Stanick Jeannette

Emanuel Sandhu

Yunfei Li

Chengjiang Li

Stefan Lindemann

Alexander Abt

Ben Ferreira

No sport has jumped forward so quickly as men's figure skating has. And this comes from guys who spend most of their time going backwards.

Kurt Browning, the man who landed the world's first quadruple jump in 1988, didn't even need one to win his four world titles before turning pro in 1994. Even as late as December 1997 at the Grand Prix Final in Hamilton, Ontario,

there were a total of just three quads landed by the same flight of skaters (and this was a first!). One of them was Elvis Stojko's quad/triple, the first in skating history.

But by 1999, American Tim Goebel had landed three quads by himself in the same program. In 2001, new world champion Evgeny Plushenko raised the bar with a quad/triple/double combination which inspired other elite skaters to frantically practice the nine-rotation set during the off-season.

At 2001 Worlds, just 39 months after Stojko unleashed the first quad/triple combination, there were five of them landed in the short program, six more in the freeskate and many, many others attempted. Plushenko and Tim Goebel were also predicting that they would eventually do all six

recognized jumps as quadruples.

"With the jumping and improved presentation," says Alexei Yagudin, "you really, really have to work to be in the top group."

Yagudin's done a pretty good job of that, winning three straight Worlds before finishing second to Plushenko's magnificent performance in 2001. But despite his spectacular record when it counted most, Yagudin didn't always dominate during the season, emphasizing just how deep the men's field has become.

Additionally, the roster is no longer divided into jumpers and artists.

Plushenko is one of the most captivating performers in the sport, with interesting spins and long lines, and is

also one of the best jumpers. Canadian Emanuel Sandhu, a throwback to a more balletic era, has become a sudden challenger by perfecting his quad/triple. Japan's Yamato Tamura is so electrifying he has a rock-star appeal in his home country. More purely athletic types, such as Yagudin, Stojko and Michael Weiss, have matured and found perfect choreographic vehicles, most often in blockbuster-movie themes. Many of those who find themselves just out of reach of the podium—Goebel, and a host of Chinese skaters—do so because their presentation, not their athleticism, is still developing.

"You have got to have the whole package now to win this thing," says prominent coach Doug Leigh.

Still, Todd Eldredge won a bronze medal at 2001 Worlds without attempting a quad, and his long-time rival Stojko won a silver the year before when he missed his. They had other strong assets to fall back upon.

Eldredge, at 29, became the oldest skater to win a world medal in 70 years. Stojko was 28 when he won his silver the season before. Many other top-10 contenders are in their 20s, so there is a maturity level in men's skating which didn't exist in the past. That, in turn, has increased the entertainment quotient. But there is also a heavy emphasis on youth. Plushenko and Yagudin won Worlds while still in their teens.

The rivalry between Plushenko and Yagudin is obvious, although both claim it isn't bitter. In any case, the two of them disproved the theory that Russian skating would wither when the Soviet Union collapsed in 1992. If anything, it's become stronger. Including Yagudin and Plushenko, Russian men won four world junior titles in six years and four straight Worlds. As Alexander Abt, ranked eighth in the world, can attest, sometimes it's harder to place well at Russian Nationals than at Worlds.

The same could be said for the men's division's fastest-rising country. China's Zhengxin Guo was the first man to land two quads in the same program in 1997, finished eighth at 2000 Worlds and couldn't even make the world team for 2001. Yunfei Li finished only fourth at Chinese Nationals in 2001 but was sixth at Worlds. The winners of the men's Junior Grand Prix Final in 2000 and 2001 were both Chinese.

And of the seven quads successfully landed in the short program at 2001 Worlds, three were by the Chinese men and a fourth was by Australia's Anthony Liu, who was trained in China. The Chinese moved all their skaters to a training center in Beijing two years prior to Salt Lake, to prepare for the Olympics.

The Chinese have never won a world medal in men's, however, they're knocking on the door. But it's a very crowded house. In the 2001-02 season, men's skating saw a rarity: four different world champions—Stojko, Eldredge, Yagudin and Plushenko—were registered for the Grand Prix circuit. And there were at least five other skaters who were considered serious medal threats

The men's division is not only reaching new heights, it has new-found depth.

Evgeny Plushenko

He is "The Natural."

Evgeny Plushenko landed his first triple jump when he was seven years old, and had all six triples mastered by the time he was 13. He was also the first man to do the aching Biellmann spin, and the first to do a quad/triple/double combination, the highlight of his championship freeskate at 2001 Worlds.

So there is no reason to doubt his chances of achieving his next goal.

"My dream is to do all jumps as quad jumps, even the Axel," Plushenko says. "Every skater wants to do something better, to improve on himself."

Plushenko's been doing that since he was four years old in the southern Russian industrial city of Volgograd. From the first stroke on the ice he was a rarity: a male skater with flexibility, unlimited athletic potential and an innate sense of showmanship. "The Natural." It was just a matter of time, and coaching, until he conquered the world.

As a very young child, Plushenko suffered from bleeding noses and his worried mother, Tatiana, took him to the skating arena, where she had friends, in the hope that his health would improve.

"She said I could skate for fun not for gold medals," he recalls. "Then I won my first competition when I was seven and she said 'Wow! Maybe now you can skate for medals!'"

She also said that he could do the back-breaking Biellmann spin he had admired a young female skater performing, but only if he practiced it every day, which she made sure he did. He eventually became the first man to do one in competition and it is now his signature move.

Although Plushenko has been coached by the colorful Alexei Mishin since 1994, his first serious coach was a weightlifter, which explains the incredible power in his jumps. But when he was 11, and the old Soviet Union was in shambles, the arena in Volgograd was turned into a car dealership. He and his mother left his father and sister at home and traveled north to Mishin's famous St. Petersburg school where Olympic champion Alexei Urmanov and Plushenko's future rival Alexei Yagudin were already training.

In a description which would become famous in the skating world, Mishin recalled Plushenko's arrival in St. Petersburg. "He looked like a cheap chicken, very green and very blue and no fat...very ecological."

Born: November 3, 1982, Solnechi, Russia

Hometown: St. Petersburg

Training Site: St. Petersburg

Coach: Alexei Mishin

Choreographers: Edward Smirnov, David Audish

RESULTS

1998: 3rd Worlds
2nd Europeans
1st Skate Canada
2nd Cup of Russia
3rd Goodwill Games
3rd Russian Nationals

1999: 2nd Worlds
3rd Grand Prix Final
2nd Europeans
1st NHK
1st Cup of Russia
1st Sparkassen Cup
1st Russian Nationals

2000: 4th Worlds
1st Grand Prix Final
1st Europeans
1st NHK
1st Sparkassen Cup
1st Cup of Russia
1st Russian Nationals

2001: 1st Worlds
1st Grand Prix Final
1st Europeans
1st Russian Nationals

Worlds | Vancouver | March 2001

• Evgeny has said he wants to be World, Olympic and European Champion, "and not just one time."

And very poor. Plushenko and his mother shared a small apartment with another family and Mishin had to pay most of the rent. His family's financial problems provided motivation for Plushenko to train hard every day. He wanted to skate well enough to win prize money to

help his family buy an apartment, a dream he eventually realized. His mother and father now live in a large apartment with his two dogs, an American bulldog and an Indian bulldog.

When Plushenko was 14, he landed his first quad and only 10 days later had his first quad/triple combination. At the same time, he was developing the intricate spins which only a skater of his flexibility could master.

"He can do the Biellmann in both directions, but doesn't need that right now," Mishin said at 2001 Worlds. "I didn't do anything for that flexibility, he had it when he came to me because his mother pushed and pulled him to get it."

Quips Plushenko, "Thank you mummy."

In 1997, just three years after arriving in St. Petersburg, Plushenko won the world junior title. Later that year, he made his Grand Prix debut, finishing second to Todd Eldredge at Skate America. He was European silver medalist a few months later, but was left off the Russian Olympic team in favor of Yagudin and eventual gold medalist Ilia Kulik. He was back on the team for Worlds a month after the Olympics and made a stunning debut. He had a chance to win but fell three times as he began to ad-lib his freeskate program under pressure. Still, he won a bronze medal, a spectacular achievement for a 15-year-old in his first Worlds.

The next year, he moved up to second and at 2000 Worlds, Plushenko seemed poised to become the youngest men's champion in history. He'd had a superb season, winning every

event he entered, including Europeans. But he was still only 17, and lost his poise in the freeskate, finishing a disappointing fourth.

"I learned from that," he said the next season. "I was thinking just about medals. So now, I just skate, I don't think about medals. I think just about jumps."

He got bigger and stronger over the summer—"I grew up," he said—and ripped through the 2000–01 season winning all but one of his events. This time there was no stopping him at Worlds. He used a different freeskate program for the qualifying rounds and final, the first person ever to do so, and led the competition from wire to wire. No one was even close. The only reason he didn't earn a

slew of 6.0s for his freeskate is that there were a couple of top skaters yet to perform.

"One day years ago I was watching TV with my parents and Victor Petrenko won the world championship," Plushenko recalled. "I said 'I want to skate the same, and to win the Worlds.' So my dreams came true."

And TV is exactly where his mother watched his dreams come true. She has never seen her son at a live competition, even at events held in St. Petersburg.

"That started when I was young," Plushenko says. "And I think we will keep it that way."

Why not? It's working.

Alexei Yagudin

Alexei Yagudin won three straight world championships, but the one he lost might have been his greatest victory.

Yagudin finished second at the 2001 Worlds to his former training partner Evgeny Plushenko, who cruised through the week 10 feet tall and bulletproof.

But it was Yagudin's vulnerability, and his eventual triumph over it, which earned him the adoration of the capacity crowds.

While running near his Connecticut home a week before he was scheduled to leave for the Worlds in Vancouver, Yagudin noticed an ache in his right foot. By his 21st birthday, the day before the men's qualifying round, the ache had graduated to severe pain and he considered withdrawing.

Skating fans, so accustomed to seeing Yagudin rise to the occasion, had no idea he was injured and therefore had no idea why he stumbled through the qualifying round. He landed only his triple flip and two triple Axels and fell twice. He finished a disastrous fifth in his group, dashing his hopes not only of a fourth consecutive title, but perhaps of even a medal X-rays later revealed a heavy build-up of fluid between the bones of his right foot and doctors told him he should drop out.

"I sat in my room crying sometimes from the pain," Yagudin explained. He decided to soldier on, and before the short program, two nights later, reminded himself "I didn't win three world titles by accident. I think people show their best results when they are hurt, like Elvis did in Nagano."

So, with the pain temporarily dulled by two injections of a local anesthetic, he landed a quadruple toe loop/triple toe loop combination to open his short program and collected a raucous standing ovation. He repeated the injections, the combination, and the ovation, in his famous Gladiator freeskate program to complete the comeback for the silver medal. But the physical stress had taken its toll. The injury worsened, and he was forced to skip the Skate the Nation tour through Canada.

"I wanted to prove that I'm a fighter and a good skater," Yagudin said afterward.

He didn't have much to prove.

Born: March 18, 1980, Leningrad, Soviet Union

Hometown: St. Petersburg, Russia

Training Site: Newington, Connecticut

Coach: Tatiana Tarasova

Choreographer: Vladimir Ullanov

RESULTS

1998: 5th Olympics
1st Worlds

1999: 1st Worlds
1st Europeans
1st Skate Canada
1st Trophee Lalique

2000: 1st Worlds
2nd Europeans
1st Skate Canada
1st Trophee Lalique
2nd Skate America
1st Japan Open

2001: 2nd Worlds
2nd Europeans
2nd Grand Prix Final
1st Japan Open

• Alexei has won three world titles but never the Russian Championships. He has finished second four times.

Worlds | Vancouver | March 2001

Worlds | Vancouver | March 2001

Skate Canada | Mississauga | November 2000
Though props are forbidden in competition, Alexei uses real knives when he skates his dramatic free program in exhibition!

In 1998, just two weeks after his 18th birthday, Yagudin became the second-youngest men's gold medalist in the 102-year history of the world championship. (Canada's Don McPherson was a week younger when he won in 1963.) He is the only man to win three straight titles without support of the compulsory figures, which were abolished in 1990. And 2001 wasn't the first time he'd shown his warrior side. At the 1998 Olympics, he finished fifth despite skating with flu and a high fever. Because of political in-fighting, he was left off the Russian team for the 1998 Worlds, but was reinstated two weeks before the event. Then, a couple of days before skating, he came down with food poisoning, and still won his first title. In 2000, he crashed into the boards during practice and broke a metacarpal bone 12 days before the European championships. He arrived with his hand in a cast, but won the short program and finished second overall. A month later, just after his 20th birthday, he won his third straight world title.

The international skating community first took notice of Yagudin when, as a high-spirited 14-year-old, he finished fourth at the 1994 Junior Worlds. He was training in St. Petersburg, Russia with Plushenko and '94 Olympic champion Alexei Urmanov under master coach Alexei Mishin.

When Yagudin was born, Russia was still under the Soviet Union's communist system and St. Petersburg was known as Leningrad. Under that regime, skating lessons were provided free, and when Yagudin was four-and-a-half his mother Zoya decided to register him, "just to keep me busy." His parents divorced when Alexei was 10, and his father Konstantin left for Germany. He hasn't talked to his father since, a separation which bothers him, "but my mother has been both mother and father to me. She did a lot for me."

Zoya, Alexei and his grandmother Maria lived in a small apartment, which they had to share with another family (a mother and her son) whom they didn't know.

"Four rooms. Same bathroom, same kitchen, for both families. My family was poor. It was a really tough time for me. I was just skating, skating, skating and then I started to earn some money from figure skating and I was like, 'Wow!'. First, I was buying a lot of clothes and other stuff for my family. When I was able to buy a flat for my family, I did right away. I'm really glad that you can make money in skating now, not just to help me, but also to help my family. Because without them I would be no one."

Yagudin left Mishin, and St. Petersburg, after he won his first world championship to train with skating's grande dame Tatiana Tarasova, who had just moved to the U.S.A. He felt Mishin was too much of a disciplinarian and was favoring his younger star, Plushenko. That started a long-running public

Worlds | Vancouver | March 2001   Worlds | Vancouver | March 2001

rivalry between the two former clubmates but Yagudin says, "We can talk. I think we can describe it like Kwan and Lipinski."

Tarasova added a soft, artistic touch to Yagudin's powerful technical arsenal and by the time he had won his second world title in 1999, he had developed into skating's coveted "complete package." Though three times world champion, paradoxically he has never won his national title, which remains a goal. After the 2002 Olympics he might not compete as much as in the past, but says he's committed to skate in every Russian, European and World Championship until the 2006 Olympics.

"Before I was thinking just about titles and not about people. I was just going to win," he explains. "Now, everything has changed. It's still important to win, but it's not just a competition, it's an event. Like a huge holiday for me.

"But I do want to win the Olympics, that's what matters most."

Yagudin spends most of his year in Newington, Connecticut, where he plays tennis every day after practice in the off-season. His mother comes to visit for several months each year. Otherwise, he shares his apartment with his cocker spaniel Lawrie, named after Lawrence of Arabia, one of his most memorable freeskate programs.

Because he's so fond of North American fans, he may eventually take out an American or Canadian passport, "but I will always be Russian in my soul." Still, he feels he doesn't get enough respect in his homeland, and isn't afraid to say so. That outspokenness, combined with his sense of humor and diverse array of skating skills, have won over the North American media.

And his willingness to fight through pain has won over everybody else.

Todd Eldredge

In any other walk of life, Todd Eldredge would be considered a young man. But in figure skating, where world championships are won at 18 and professional careers bloom at 25, he is as ancient as the pharaohs.

"When I skate against Alexei Yagudin or Evgeny Plushenko, I don't think of myself as being the old guy—I think of myself as being the experienced guy," says Eldredge, who came back from a two-year absence to win a world championshp bronze in 2001.

That seasoning figured prominently in the 2001 Worlds, where Eldredge kept using a metaphor from golf, the other sport at which he excels.

"You play the course, you don't play the other guy," he said. "I try to shoot par, and if the other guys shoot bogeys, I'm okay."

Eldredge means that while he may not possess as much firepower as some of the young lords a-leapin'—his only quad isn't fully consistent—he tries to perform everything he has, flawlessly, seamlessly and with flourish. If other skaters crash while attempting more difficult tricks, the strength of Eldredge's overall skating leaves him in a favorable position.

That strategy worked brilliantly at his comeback Worlds. Knowing that many others before him had fallen, Eldredge opted to skip the quad in the short program, relying upon a perfect triple Axel/triple toe loop combination. His execution was so skilled, his final spin so electric, that the audience was on its feet before the music ended. He finished fourth in the short, leaving him within a strong freeskate of the podium. He delivered that too, earning another standing ovation and a bronze medal.

In the quad squad era, Eldredge had reached the podium without attempting a four-rotation jump, proving that there is still a place for spins, exemplary triples, a refined program and elegant, comprehensive, skating.

And it proved that age doesn't have to be an insurmountable barrier. Eldredge was more than eight years senior to the other top-five finishers. At 29, he had become the oldest men's world championship medal winner in 70 years. American Roger Turner was 30 when he took a silver in 1931.

Life had certainly come full cycle for Eldredge since 1990, when he became the youngest American champion in 24 years.

Born: August 28, 1971, Chatam, Massachusetts

Hometown: Chatam, Massachusetts

Training Site: Bloomfield Hills, Michigan

Coach: Richard Callaghan

Choreographers: Kirk Wyse, Igor Shpilband

Worlds | Vancouver | March 2001

RESULTS

1997: 2nd Worlds
2nd Grand Prix Final
1st Skate America
4th Trophee Lalique
1st U.S. Nationals

1998: 4th Olympics
2nd Worlds
3rd Grand Prix Final
1st Goodwill Games
1st Masters of Skating
1st U.S. Nationals

1999: 3rd Japan Open
1st Sears Open
4th Skate Canada

2000: 2nd Japan Open
3rd Skate America
2nd Skate Canada

2001: 3rd Worlds
3rd Japan Open
2nd U.S. Nationals

• Todd volunteers many hours to work with the Blind and Handicapped Skating Association.

Skate Canada | Mississauga | November 2000
Todd's skating always carries great feeling and intensity.

Champions on Ice | Detroit | November 1999   Skate Canada | St. John | November 1998

"When I first arrived, I was known as the guy who had the jumps and not the artistry," Eldredge said, marveling at the irony. "And now it's kind of come around the other way. The guy who can-he-do-the-quad, but has got the artistry."

Eldredge's bronze was his sixth world medal and came a full decade after his first one. It was an unexpectedly successful start to a comeback designed to fill the one gap in his skating resume. He has won a world championship, five American crowns, the U.S. novice and junior titles and a few "open" championships, but he has never won an Olympic medal. After just missing, with a disappointing fourth-place finish at Nagano in 1998, he retained his eligibility but for two seasons didn't compete at Nationals or Worlds, concentrating instead on touring. He rejoined the international circuit in 2000–01, building steadily toward the Salt Lake City Games.

The Olympics have been on his mind since he began skating at the age of five in the small Cape Cod town of Chatam, Massachusetts, where his mother is a nurse and his father a commercial fisherman who gets up every morning at 4 a.m. to sail 30 miles out into the Atlantic. For nine years, the townspeople of Chatam held an annual clambake to help fund Eldredge's skating career and in 1997, he paid them back with a donation to the town. A civic ballpark is named in his honor. He is one of the most modest, friendly, helpful men in skating, traits he attributes to his hometown.

Eldredge left Chatam as a 10-year-old to follow coach Richard Callaghan to several postings, finally landing in Bloomfield Hills, Michigan. By 1990, he was U.S. champion and fifth in the world. A year later, he won his first medal, a bronze, and the future seemed golden.

But then adversity struck. A misaligned spinal joint sidelined him for most of the next season, including the 1992 Nationals, but he was given an exemption berth on the Olympic team. Battling back problems he missed a routine double Axel in the Olympic short program and finished 10th overall. He felt he had lost favor with the

Worlds | Vancouver | March 2001
One of the fastest and best spins in the world.

U.S. Figure Skating Association, and his confidence vanished. When he finished a dismal sixth at the 1993 U.S. Nationals, he seriously considered quitting the sport. But another Winter Games was scheduled for 1994, and he committed himself to making the U.S. team. He was skating well when he was stricken by flu and fever during Nationals. He finished a devastating fourth and didn't qualify for the Lillehammer Olympics.

Eldredge didn't want to end his amateur career on that disappointing note, and rededicated himself to skating. By the next spring he had regained his U.S. title, the first American skater to spend three years off the podium then come back to reclaim the championship. He proved the comeback was no fluke when he won a silver medal at Worlds, then won the 1996 world championship with an emotional performance at Edmonton. When he won

silver again at '97 Worlds, he seemed well positioned for that elusive Olympic medal. But he was fourth at Nagano, prompting the two-year layoff and his second major comeback, this time for the 2002 Games. A month into his return, at the Masters of Figure Skating, he became the oldest man to successfully land a quad.

"In those few years off, I didn't really do a lot of ISU-style freeskates," he said. "So getting back into that was probably the hardest part. I think it was the best thing for my skating, though. I think I've improved my skating, made up a lot of what I lost the last couple of years. It's a good start to be ready for Salt Lake.

"I don't feel like I've accomplished what I'd like to at the Olympics. I've accomplished pretty much everything else."

And then some.

Elvis Stojko

Exhausted, Elvis Stojko sat in the Kiss 'n' Cry, looked directly into the camera and said, "I'm sorry."

There was nothing to be sorry for.

The seven-time champion may have been heading for a career-worst 10th-place finish at 2001 Worlds, but hundreds of thousands of skating fans, watching on television, felt he had no reason to apologize. Elvis Stojko had already given them far more than they had ever anticipated.

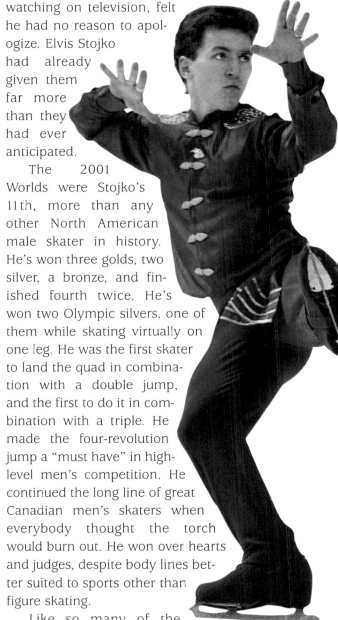

The 2001 Worlds were Stojko's 11th, more than any other North American male skater in history. He's won three golds, two silver, a bronze, and finished fourth twice. He's won two Olympic silvers, one of them while skating virtually on one leg. He was the first skater to land the quad in combination with a double jump, and the first to do it in combination with a triple. He made the four-revolution jump a "must have" in high-level men's competition. He continued the long line of great Canadian men's skaters when everybody thought the torch would burn out. He won over hearts and judges, despite body lines better suited to sports other than figure skating.

Like so many of the movie-theme characters he portrays on the ice, he has faced great challenges and stared them down.

"One thing I'm proud of is that I've done it my way," Stojko says. "I've been true to myself the whole time and

Born: March 22, 1972, Newmarket, Ontario

Hometown: Richmond Hill, Ontario

Training Site: Aston, Pennsylvania

Coach: Uschi Keszler

Choreographer: Uschi Keszler

RESULTS

1990: 9th Worlds
2nd Canadian Nationals

1991: 6th Worlds
1st Skate Canada
2nd Canadian Nationals

1992: 7th Olympics
3rd Worlds
1st Skate Canada
2nd NHK
2nd Canadian Nationals

1993: 2nd Worlds
1st Piruetten
2nd Canadian Nationals

1994: 2nd Olympics
1st Worlds
1st Skate Canada
1st Nations Cup
1st Canadian Nationals

1995: 1st Worlds
1st NHK
3rd Trophee de France

1996: 4th Worlds
2nd Grand Prix Final
1st NHK
1st Skate Canada
1st Canadian Nationals

1997: 1st Worlds
1st Skate Canada
1st Sparkassen Cup
1st Canadian Nationals

1998: 2nd Olympics
2nd Grand Prix Final
1st Canadian Nationals

1999: 4th Worlds
3rd Four Continents
2nd Skate Canada
2nd Skate America
1st Canadian Nationals

2000: 2nd Worlds
2nd Grand Prix Final
1st Four Continents
1st Canadian Nationals

2001: 10th Worlds

- Elvis was the first man to do a quad/double, and the first man to do a quad/triple.

- Says fellow three-time world champion Alexei Yagudin, "I would like, sometime in my life, to be a hero like Elvis is in his country."

- Received Meritorious Service Cross from Canada's Governor-General for contribution to sport.

Elvis personifies the true spirit of competition. He is capable of the most extraordinary performances, where we see the glory of the ultimate effort.

had some bumps along the way. But maybe those bumps were why I had impact."

Stojko's father Steve was born in Slovenia, the eldest of 10 children. His mother Irene, the youngest of nine, escaped Hungary after the 1956 revolution. When they met in Canada, Elvis Presley was still in his prime, so when their third, and final, child was born they named him after the King of Rock 'n' Roll. They couldn't have known he would become the King of Skating.

Stojko began skating at the age of five in Richmond Hill, a small town north of Toronto, Ontario. From the first day, he demonstrated a strong sense of balance and a desire to be airborne, traits that would lead him to his other two favorite sports: martial arts and dirt-biking.

When he was seven, his parents bought him a mini-cycle to ride around the family farm. He now owns several motorcycles and could probably win championships if he raced, rather than rode for relaxation.

His father put Elvis in karate classes at seven so he could defend himself. At 16, Stojko earned a black belt, but it was the mental aspects of the sport which influenced him most. He liked its mental discipline and spiritual awareness and put both to use in his skating career.

At 13, Stojko moved from Richmond Hill to Barrie to train with Doug Leigh, who was soon to take Brian Orser

to Canada's first men's world championship in a quarter-century. Stojko watched Orser's training dedication, copied it and improved upon it. Orser didn't do the world's first triple Axel—fellow Canadian Vern Taylor did—but he perfected it. Likewise, Stojko didn't do the world's first quadruple jump—fellow Canadian Kurt Browning did—but he perfected it.

And in 1991 he made the history books himself, landing the first quadruple/double combination at the world championship. Six years later he landed the world's first quad/triple at the Grand Prix Final.

Despite his technical prowess, Stojko had trouble swaying judges who didn't like his artistry, preferring the longer, sleeker lines of classic men's skaters. But he perservered with his masculine style, and his firm belief that, "I don't want to use gimmicks, I skate who I am." He found appropriate vehicles in masculine movie themes: *Robin Hood*, *Merlin*, *Gladiator*. He won a bronze at the '92 Worlds, a silver in 1993 and, finally, a month after he won a silver at the 1994 Olympics, he was world champion, earning the first 6.0 given to a men's skater for technical elements since 1980.

In 1995 he won the world championship again, just a month after severely torn ankle ligaments forced him out of Canadian Nationals. He won those Worlds skating with dreadful pain, but that was nothing compared to the physical agony of the 1998 Olympics. During the Nagano Games, Stojko was skating with torn groin muscles which made it difficult to walk, let alone skate. Only his coaches knew of his terrible injury, and somehow he managed to finish second in the short program and land eight triples in the long. When it was over he was rushed to the Olympic hospital in agony, unaware that he had hung on to win a silver medal.

"When you consider the conditions, that was the best performance I've ever done," he would say years later.

The injury forced Stojko to miss half a year of training. He returned to finish fourth at the 1999 Worlds. A month later, seeking a change for change's sake, he left Leigh, his coach and friend, after 14 years together, and moved to Aston, Pennsylvania, to train with his choreographer Uschi Keszler. At 2000 Worlds, eight days after his 28th birthday, he won a silver medal, completing the long, difficult climb back to the podium.

Because of four separate injuries, that would be the last time he would compete until the 2001 Worlds. He feels the lack of competitive "mileage" explained his rough week in Vancouver, and it did not alter his determination to compete at the 2002 Olympics, his fourth Games.

"I didn't stay in this for three years to get out because I didn't deliver at Worlds," he explained. "When I chose to stay eligible after 1998, I knew I'd have to go through more criticism, people saying I'm too old.

"But then, I'm always the one who has done things differently."

Canadians | Ottawa | February 1999

Elvis Tour | Toronto | September 1998
Elvis' exhibition routines are always fun, but he saves his "Elvis Routine" for special performances.

Takeshi Honda

It's fortunate for Japanese figure skating that the little things—toe picks, for instance—don't discourage Takeshi Honda.

"The first day I figure skated, I caught the toe pick, fell forward, and went right onto the ice," the effervescent Honda recalls with a laugh.

When he made that rookie face-plant, Honda was nine years old, and trying to make some sense out of those unfamiliar boots and blades. For two years, he'd been a short-track speed skater like his brother.

By the time he was 14, Honda had become the youngest-ever Japanese champion, and at 15, he was landing quadruple toe loops in practice. Between 1996 and 2001, he failed to win the national senior championship only twice, both times when he was forced to withdraw with injury.

In late 1997, Honda moved to Simsbury, Connecticut, to work with Victor Petrenko's coach Galina Zmievskaya. Earlier that year he had finally met, and had his picture taken with, his idol Kurt Browning during the World Championships in Edmonton. But the two didn't have a conversation, because Honda couldn't speak a word of English. He decided to rectify the situation by leaving Japan.

"Most Japanese skaters just stick with our own team, because they don't speak English," Honda said during the 2001 Worlds. "I've been over here four years in row. I changed everything. I have a lot of new friends."

He returned to Japan a few months later for the 1998 Winter Olympics at Nagano. Nerve-wracked and carrying the burden of national expectations, he did not skate well and finished a disappointing 15th.

"At that point I was thinking that maybe I would stop skating. But I decided I had changed everything in my life and I just said, 'Four more years I will try this.'"

A month after the Olympics he landed his first quad at a World Championship, during the qualifying round. By November, he had moved from Connecticut to the Mariposa skating club in Ontario, Canada.

Elvis Stojko was at Mariposa in those days, and Honda absorbed some of the three-time world champion's grit. In 1999, he captured the inaugural Four Continents Championship, finishing first in the short program and holding off Stojko in the freeskate, having just recovered from an ankle injury. He also turned in an impressive sixth-place finish at Worlds. Although Honda has not yet realized

Born: March 23, 1981, Koriyama, Fukushima

Hometown: Koriyama, Fukushima

Training Site: Barrie, Ontario

Coach: Doug Leigh

Choreographer: Lori Nichol

RESULTS

1998: 15th Olympics
11th Worlds

1999: 6th Worlds
1st Four Continents

2000: 10th Worlds
5th Four Continents

2001: 5th Worlds
2nd Four Continents

his full potential, his coach Doug Leigh says, "We've got everything on track now. It's right there." In 2001 at the Worlds he finished fifth, his best world ranking in six appearances.

Worlds | Vancouver | March 2001

- Canadian figure skating fans have developed an allegiance to Honda. They've adopted him as one of their own.

Worlds | Vancouver
March 2001

Four Continents | Salt Lake City
February 2001

Virtuosity on ice: Takeshi delivers great style with great musicality.

Tim Goebel

When people say that Tim Goebel has jumped into the world's top five, that's exactly what they mean.

There is no metaphor here. Goebel himself knows that it is his jumps, his quadruples in particular, which have accelerated him through the ranks. While he is still developing his artistic components, Goebel owns the quad Salchow. He was the first skater to do a quadruple Salchow, the first to do it in combination, the first American to do a quad of any kind and the first skater to include three quads in the same program. He accomplished the latter in winning a silver medal at Skate America at Colorado Springs in 1999.

"I think that was really my breakthrough into the uppercrust of the skating world," Goebel says. "It was the first time I'd won a medal at an international of such high caliber."

It would not be his last. Goebel won a bronze later that season at the Grand Prix Final. And he narrowly missed the podium at 2001 Worlds, finishing fourth, seven spots better than the previous year's result.

Goebel started skating at four in a Chicago suburb, and began serious training when he was 10, moving to Lakewood, Illinois, to work with coaches Glyn Watts and Carol Heiss-Jenkins. By 1994 he was U.S. Novice champion and he eventually completed the triple crown by winning the National Junior (1996) and Senior (2001) championships. But it was in March 1998 at the Junior Grand Prix Final where Goebel really grabbed the spotlight. Fourth after the short program, he landed the world's first quadruple Salchow in the freeskate to claim his first international victory.

"My first reaction was relief because I needed it to win," he said. "But I was also proud to be the first American to land a quad. I'd worked on it for about three years."

Goebel now trains in California. He works with brilliant choreographer Lori Nichol and takes ballet to enhance his artistic qualities.

"It's a really different way of thinking, not just to go out there and do jumps," Goebel says. "It's a develop-

| **Born:** September, 10, 1980, Evanston, Illinois |
| **Hometown:** Rolling Meadows, Illinois |
| **Training Site:** El Segundo, California |
| **Coach:** Frank Carroll |
| **Choreographer:** Lori Nichol |

RESULTS

1999: 12th Worlds
13th Four Continents
2nd Skate America
2nd NHK
3rd U.S. Nationals

2000: 11th Worlds
3rd Grand Prix Final
2nd Sparkassen Cup
1st Skate America
2nd U.S. Nationals

2001: 4th Worlds
5th Grand Prix Final
1st U.S. Nationals

Worlds | Vancouver | March 2001

• Tim was on the honor roll at school from 1992–99 and considered studying medicine.

mental process. You don't just become artistic. I'm a little bit ahead in the jumping now, and I always want to keep that edge on everybody. But I want to improve my artistry so that it's even stronger than my technical."

He's heading down the right road.

Michael Weiss

It seems inevitable that Michael Weiss would become a world-class athlete.

His sister Geremi was silver medalist at the 1990 U.S. Junior Nationals; his other sister, Genna, was world junior diving champion. His mother Margie was a collegiate gymnastics champion and is a fitness instructor. And his father Greg competed at the 1964 Olympics in Japan as a gymnast. So when Weiss qualified for the 1998 Winter Olympics in Japan, he felt like he'd upheld family tradition. "It's kind of like the circle of life coming back around," he said at the time.

Weiss is an athletic, mature, all-round skater who, like Elvis Stojko, wants to bring an aggressive, "masculine" style to the sport.

Weiss was a regional diving champion and began skating at the relatively late age of nine, and he's had the same coach, Audrey Weisiger, since then. At 17 he was world junior champ. Weiss won his first national senior title in 1999, with an eight-triple performance, and a month later landed his first clean quad at Worlds, and won a bronze medal.

Born: August 2, 1976, Washington, D.C.

Hometown: Fairfax, Virginia

Training Site: Fairfax, Virginia

Coach: Audrey Weisiger

Choreographers: Brian Wright, Lisa Thornton-Weiss.

RESULTS

1998: 7th Olympics
6th Worlds
4th Goodwill Games
2nd Skate America
2nd Canadian Open
2nd Trophee Lalique
2nd U.S. Nationals

1999: 3rd Worlds
4th Grand Prix Final
4th Skate America
5th Trophee Lalique
1st U.S. Nationals

2000: 3rd Worlds
7th Cup of Russia
1st U.S. Nationals

2001: 3rd Four Continents
4th U.S. Nationals

Four Continents | Salt Lake City | February 2001

Worlds | Nice | March 2000

Clean lines refine Michael's powerful performances.

• Michael almost became the first American to land a quad, at the 1997 U.S. Nationals. Study of video replays detected it was slightly "two-footed."

It's a testament to that country's skating depth that in 2001 a sub-par Weiss could not make the American team for Worlds despite being two-time defending national champion and twice a Worlds bronze medalist.

The setback would only motivate Weiss, who is among the most confident skaters in the U.S. and who also has a strong support system at home in his wife and two small children. "I go back to the house from the rink and I still have to change diapers. It keeps me well-grounded. It keeps me focused on the things in life that really count," says Weiss, who was voted 1999 Father of the Year by the National Fatherhood Initiative.

Stanick Jeannette

Potential can be a heavy burden, especially if it takes years to turn into reality.

Stanick Jeannette, the entertaining, innovative skater from the northwestern Paris suburb of Cergy had been viewed as a future international celebrity since he won the French junior nationals at the age of 15. But something always seemed to prevent him from attaining stardom. He had several injuries, the worst requiring surgery to a tendon in 1994. He broke a skate blade during the 1998 Nationals.

His coach Pierre Trente once said, "With Stanick you have skating in its purest form, skating with real emotion. But when is he going to get his act together?"

The correct answer was, "December 11, 1999." Jeannette won his first national senior title at the age of 22. Finally, he would represent France at Europeans and Worlds.

"I've been waiting for this for years," Jeannette said. "It seems like a door opening."

So many of those doors had closed on him before. Jeannette's role model was the inventive Canadian skater Gary Beacom, a brilliant but unorthodox performer of the 1980s and 1990s. The Beacom influence shows in Jeannette's impressive showmanship, pure body lines and creative spins. But like many artistic skaters, Jeannette was often the victim of his own emotions. A French press release once noted that in competition Jeannette would sometimes "explode in wild uncontrolled jumps."

Jeannette persevered, however, and worked with experts such as former world pairs champion Randy Gardner on edges, flow and body position. While still unpredictable, he became a little more consistent in his performances. In the winter of 2001, he won Nationals again and finished third at Europeans.

"The medal at Europeans has given me a great amount of confidence. I am feeling that the audiences and the other competitors started to see me differently, with new eyes."

The same eyes which once saw only potential.

| **Born:** March 6, 1977, Courbevoie |
| **Hometown:** Cergy |
| **Training Site:** Paris |
| **Coach:** Pierre Trente |
| **Choreographers:** Annick Gailhaguet, Sebastien Lefrancois |

RESULTS

1999: 8th Skate America
10th Sparkassen Cup
5th French Nationals

2000: 7th Worlds
9th Europeans
2nd Trophee Lalique
9th Sparkassen Cup
1st French Nationals

2001: 11th Worlds
3rd Europeans
1st French Nationals

• "Choreography is like vocabulary," Stanick says. "Sebastien Lefrancois teaches me new letters' every day."

Worlds | Vancouver | March 2001

🔺 Worlds | Vancouver | March 2001
Stan is a true innovator.

Emanuel Sandhu

Sometimes, success doesn't come until you're mature enough to accept it.

For years, everyone had expected Emanuel Sandhu to establish himself as one of the world's elite skaters. He did exactly that at the 2001 Worlds, finishing ninth overall, including a spectacular fifth-place freeskate.

"But this wasn't about redemption," Sandhu said afterwards. "It was a learning experience. It was about growing up."

There is no tougher place to grow up than on the public stage, which is where Sandhu suddenly found himself after winning a silver medal at the 1998 Nationals. It was his first year in senior and the sensational result was completely unexpected. The Canadian Olympic Association ruled that although Sandhu was the country's second-best men's skater he could not attend the Nagano Olympics because he hadn't performed in enough senior internationals. That decision caused a national uproar and threw the spotlight of controversy on an emotional teenager when he should have been quietly preparing for the Worlds.

"It was a roller coaster ride and I was too inexperienced to handle it."

Sandhu grew up in the same Toronto-area town as Elvis Stojko. Born to a Sikh father and Italian mother, his first love was ballet. At nine, he was accepted to study at the National Ballet School of Canada. A few months earlier, he had started figure skating, wearing second-hand hockey skates.

Joanne McLeod, who would become his coach, noticed him "skating like a dancer and attempting a two-foot spin, with his ankles inverting in his over-sized skates." But she recognized the enormous potential in this lithe spinner. He was supple, graceful, athletic and had an impeccable ear for music. Five years after discovering figure skating, he was the Canadian novice silver medalist. McLeod had hoped for a steady rise through the senior ranks, so Sandhu could mature along the way. But an electric nine-triple freeskate at the 1998 Nationals changed that plan, and so did the Olympic eligibility battle.

Worlds | Vancouver
March 2001

| **Born:** November 18, 1980, Toronto |
| **Hometown:** Richmond Hill |
| **Training Site:** Vancouver, B.C. |
| **Coach:** Joanne McLeod |
| **Choreographer:** Joanne McLeod |

RESULTS

1999:	18th Worlds		6th Sparkassen Cup
	10th Four Continents		2nd Canadian Nationals
	8th Sparkassen Cup	**2001:**	9th Worlds
	2nd Canadian Nationals		7th Four Continents
2000:	13th Four Continents		1st Canadian Nationals
	4th Skate America		

- Emanuel's balletic style and artistic temperament lead to frequent comparisons with legendary creative forces Toller Cranston and John Curry. Cranston designed Sandhu's 2001 freeskate costume.

He struggled at his first two Worlds, then was left off the 2000 World team altogether. After some soul-searching, and moving to Vancouver, Sandhu has renewed his dedication to his sport.

His freeskate to "Journey of Man" by Cirque du Soleil won him his first Canadian senior championship in 2001. Following that with a ninth at Worlds, it was clear he had become mature enough to accept his success. "I understand I can be one of the world's best," Sandhu says. "I'm aware of my talent, and if I put it all together, good things will happen."

Worlds | Vancouver | March 2001
Emanuel's elegance is owed to the discipline of ballet.

Yunfei Li

When the first strains of Shostakovich's "King Lear" began, most of the 15,000 people in Vancouver's GM Place had never heard of the skater in front of them.

Within two minutes, they were on their feet, saluting the tenacity of this unknown soldier.

Just one minute and 49 seconds into his first performance at a world championship—the qualifying round of the 2001 Worlds—Li had run into one of the worst obstacles a competitor can face. His music stopped.

"So I just kept skating," he shrugged. For 15 seconds, until the referee finally got his attention and stopped him, Li skated on—without music, but with another kind of rhythmic accompaniment: the pulse of a standing ovation.

Li was permitted to resume his program from the point the music had stopped, but the magic had been lost. He struggled through his freeskating program and qualified sixth in his group, equivalent to a tie for 10th overall.

But by the time the week was over, Li had won hearts, a sixth-place finish and a rare spot on the roster of the Exhibition Gala which concludes a world championship.

Li's week was highlighted by a fifth-place finish in the short program and successful quadruple toe/triple toe combinations in the qualifying round and short program. Only one other skater—Tim Goebel of the U.S., with three—landed more quads at the 2001 Worlds.

For a boy who started skating because he was "sick and weak all the time," as he puts it, it was an extraordinary accomplishment. "It's very, very exciting," Li said afterward. "It was higher than I hoped to finish.

"I want to catch up to Yagudin and Plushenko and the other good skaters. This is what my goal is for the future I will keep doing this as long as possible."

After he retires, he wants to return to school, become a coach and help spread a love for figure skating through the world's largest nation.

"Before, figure skating was not very popular in our country," Li says. "But after Chen Lu and Shen/Zhao appeared it became bigger. Our skaters are very fond of Chen Lu. She is very famous in China and in the world. I want to catch up to her."

He's made a good start.

Worlds | Vancouver
March 2001

Worlds | Vancouver | March 2001
Yunfei has extreme agility.

Born: June 11, 1979; Harbin, China
Hometown: Harbin, China
Training Site: Harbin
Coach: Tian Quiusheng
Choreographer: Renee Roca

RESULTS

1994: 7th World Juniors	**2000:** 11th Four Continents
1998: 3rd World Juniors	2nd Finlandia Trophy
8th Goodwill Games	**2001:** 6th Worlds
1999: 1st Winter	8th Four Continents
Universiade	

- Nearly two years before the 2002 Olympics the Chinese moved their team to Beijing to train. Yunfei's roomate there is Chengiang Li.

Chengjiang Li

When he was five years old and living in the northern Chinese city of Changchun, Chengjiang Li saw a seven-year-old girl gracefully stroking her way across the ice surface at a nearby outdoor rink.

At that moment Li decided that figure skating was such a beautiful sport he wanted to be part of it. The seven-year-old, from the neighboring city of Jilin, was Lu Chen, and 11 years later she became the first Chinese skater to win a world championship. The boy she inspired became the first Chinese man to win an International Skating Union championship when he captured the 2001 Four Continents title in Salt Lake City.

Li's parents were both skaters and they eventually became coaches in the figure skating boom which followed Chen's rise to international prominence. But Li is part of a boom of his own. Chinese men are taking the figure skating world by storm, and domestic competition is so fierce that Zhengxin Guo, the first skater to land two quads in a freeskate, did not make the 2001 World team.

Li first gained international notice at the 1998 world junior championships in Saint John, New Brunswick. Although he finished seventh, Li became just the second man in history, behind Elvis Stojko, to land quadruple and triple jumps in combination.

At those junior Worlds, Li displayed little showmanship, laboring with a dour sense of purpose. But American

Born: April 28, 1979, Changchun

Hometown: Changchun

Training Site: Beijing

Coach: Haijun Gao

Choreographers: Lea Ann Miller, Rene Roca

RESULTS

1999: 2nd Four Continents
5th Skate Canada
1st Chinese Nationals

2000: 5th Worlds
2nd Four Continents
3rd Sparkassen Cup
3rd NHK
9th Skate Canada
2nd Chinese Nationals

2001: 7th Worlds
1st Four Continents
1st Chinese Nationals

- With his seventh-place finish at 2001 Worlds and a sixth by Yunfei Li, Chengjiang helped China qualify three men for the Olympics.

choreographer Lea Ann Miller went to work and within a couple of years, Li's natural sense of music had become evident.

And so had his work ethic. At Skate Canada in 1999 Alexei Yagudin was at an early morning practice and marveled at Li landing quad after quad.

"I was just doing spins and a couple of steps," Yagudin said. "I was like, 'Oh my gosh, what's going on with the Chinese guys?' I think he and Timothy (Goebel) will be the skaters of the future.'"

Li had a terrible qualifying round at 2001 Worlds, but fought his way back to finish seventh overall.

"I had put too much pressure on myself in qualifying, so I got too nervous," he said. "But I learned from that, and went on."

Worlds | Vancouver | March 2001

Worlds | Vancouver | March 2001
Chengjian's kung fu form brings the mysticism of the Orient to the ice.

Stefan Lindemann

Like his skating idol Elvis Stojko, Stefan Lindemann draws inspiration from other sports. But while Stojko favors individual pursuits such as martial arts and motor-cross, Germany's top male skater has always been interested in team sports.

Lindemann began figure skating at the age of four in the East German city of Erfurt. He showed real promise, but when he was 12, he wanted to switch to hockey. Luckily for him, his mother wouldn't let him because the next year, Lindemann qualified for German Junior Nationals. He finished 11th, but the following season, he was fourth and on the way to national prominence.

Lindemann is also keenly interested in soccer and was skilled enough to play "C League," a relatively high caliber of soccer, as a youth. He credits soccer for his reputation as one of the best-conditioned athletes among elite skaters. He does cross-training in the summers, working out in Chemnitz with eminent speed skater Gunda Niemann-Stirnemann, a multiple record-holder at 3000 meters.

He is coached by Ilona Schindler, who apprenticed under legendary East German coach Jutta Muller, the woman who took Katarina Witt to two Olympic championships. By the age of 15, Lindemann was competing at senior Nationals and in 1999, he won his first international, Skate Slovenia. In 2000, he became the first German male to win the World Junior Championship. That same season, he won

Born: September 30, 1980, Erfurt
Hometown: Erfurt
Training Sites: Chemnitz and Oberstdorf
Coach: Ilona Schindler
Choreographer: Dr. Rostislav Sinitsyn

RESULTS

1999: 13th Worlds
17th Europeans
14th World Juniors
1st Skate Slovenia
5th Jr. Grand Prix Final
2nd German Nationals

2000: 14th Worlds
8th Europeans
1st World Juniors
2nd Jr. Grand Prix Final
1st German Nationals

2001: 18th Worlds

his first senior national title and finished eighth at Europeans.

Lindemann says he "tries to skate like Elvis Stojko." Like Stojko, he has had success despite a body type which is not ideal for figure skating.

He had hoped to have a quadruple jump in place for 2001 Worlds, but he missed most of the season after a terrible fall at the 2000 Sparkassen Cup in Gelsenkirchen. He had to be carried off the ice with a badly injured knee and was unable to compete in any autumn competitions, at Nationals or at Europeans. At 2001 Worlds he felt the effects of his forced absence and finished only 18th, well below his potential.

But he vowed to come back with renewed strength and confidence. Just as Stojko did. Just as any team player would.

Worlds | Vancouver | March 2001
Enthusiasm is a huge part of Stefan's appeal.

• Stefan toured Germany with Stars on Ice, receiving thunderous ovations.

Worlds | Vancouver | March 2001

Alexander Abt

One of these years, the injury gods will finally smile on Alexander Abt and let him show the world exactly what he can do.

As far back as 1993, Russian journalists were touting Abt as the next great Russian skater, but he's had misfortune after misfortune since then. Abt was named to the Russian team for 1995 Europeans, but couldn't skate because of an injured hip. Knee surgery kept him out of the Russian Nationals in 1996, and a second knee operation in late 1998 ruined the rest of that season as well.

But the most debilitating injury came at a rink in Mexico when the Russian team was on tour during the summer of 1996. The practice ice was "disgusting," Abt says, and he caught a rut, sending him into the boards. His left skate sliced into the quadriceps muscle on his right leg. He spent six months in hospital, undergoing surgery twice.

"The doctors told me I would not walk at all and there was no talk of a return to sport," Abt recalled. "I relearned to walk, then later, to stand on the skates. Like a child. That year-and-a-half was like remaking the wheel."

He also had to remake all his jumps and didn't have his triple Axel for the next season. But by 1997–98 his remarkable physical comeback was complete. He was fourth at Nationals and got a berth to his first Europeans as a last-minute replacement for Ilia Kulik. He won a bronze, to complete a Russian sweep of the men's medals. But by late December, he was back in hospital for another knee surgery.

In April 1999 Abt married former ice dancer Elena Pavlova and their son Makar was born 11 months later.

"My life will be brighter and better," he said.

And it was. The next season, he made the Grand Prix Final, won his first medal at Nationals and finished sixth in his debut at Worlds. He has a quad, but has had trouble with its consistency. When the quad isn't clean, he's carried by his renowned musicality.

Abt suffered a sinus infection during 2001 Europeans. At Worlds he was still feeling the after-effects.

"Unfortunately," he said, "I already know what it means to be unlucky. I just try to do the best that I can."

- "I owe my coach everything," Alexander says. "He supported me in tough times."

Worlds | Vancouver March 2001

Born: October 22, 1976, Moscow
Hometown: Moscow
Training Site: Moscow
Coach: Rafael Arutunian
Choreographers: Rafael Arutunian, Sergei Petukhov

RESULTS

1998: 3rd Europeans
3rd Cup of Russia
2nd Nation's Cup
4th Russian Nationals

1999: 5th Grand Prix Final
2nd Cup of Russia
6th Skate America

2000: 6th Worlds
4th Europeans
4th Grand Prix Final
4th Sparkassen Cup
5th Skate America
5th Cup of Russia
3rd Russian Nationals

2001: 8th Worlds
4th Europeans
3rd Russian Nationals

Worlds | Vancouver | March 2001
Alexander has a classical Russian style.

Ben Ferreira

Ben Ferreira was inspired to skate by watching Kurt Browning and learned to carry himself by listening to Elvis Stojko. With such impressive role models, it's little wonder that Ferreira has become one of Canada's most popular skaters although he has yet to win a national title of any kind.

Ferreira didn't take to the blades until he was 12 years old, after he had watched Browning win the 1991 World Championship on TV, reeling off triple/triple combinations. He became a member of Royal Glenora Club in Edmonton, Browning's club, and within four years he was collecting a bronze medal at novice Nationals.

By then, his career had become interwoven with Browning's. He was featured in the four-time world champion's landmark TV special, "Singin' in the Rain." And when international skating politics prevented Browning from performing the opening number at the 1996 World Championships in Edmonton, Ferreira filled in on less than 48 hours notice. His routine brought the house down.

Blessed with solid stroking and great lines, Ferreira also has a 1000-watt smile which allows a crowd to plug into him quickly. Ferreira began his long steady climb up the Canadian senior ladder with a seventh place finish in 1997. He moved up a spot each year until 2000 when he jumped onto the podium with a bronze medal, which he repeated in 2001.

Ferreira is a severe asthmatic and also suffers serious allergies. He is the national youth spokesperson for MedicAlert Foundation and hopes his success will inspire other budding athletes.

"I don't want young kids to think they're limited by anything," he said.

Four Continents | Salt Lake City | February 2001

"Mr. Cool", Ben plays his characters to perfection.

- Ben is a huge NASCAR and Formula One racing fan. He loves customized cars. He has always been coached by Jan Ullmark.

Born: April 5, 1979, Vancouver

Hometown: Edmonton

Training Site: Edmonton

Coach: Jan Ullmark

Choreographers: Ann Schelter, Mitch Millar, Kevin Cottam

RESULTS

1999: 7th Skate Canada
5th Canadian Nationals

2000: 19th Worlds
10th Four Continents
4th Skate Canada
7th NHK
3rd Canadian Nationals

2001: 9th Four Continents
3rd Canadian Nationals

Canadians | Calgary | January 2000

THE
WOMEN

Michelle Kwan

Irina Slutskaya

Sarah Hughes

Angela Nikodinov

Maria Butyrskaya

Fumie Suguri

Vanessa Gusmeroli

Elena Liashenko

Silvia Fontana

Jennifer Robinson

Mikkeline Kierkgaard

Viktoria Volchkova

Tatiana Malinina

Annie Bellemare

Over the last half-decade of the 20th Century and the early part of the 21st, there have been two dominant themes and one dominant individual in women's figure skating.

The dominant themes are age and the New Cold War between the U.S. and Russia. The dominant personality, Michelle Kwan, has been central to both.

Kwan's brilliance and consistency has earned her a spot among the all-time greats of her sport, but Kwan has also personified the demographics of her dynamic era.

She hit the world scene as a 13-year-old alternate on the U.S. team at the 1994 Olympics, won by Oksana Baiul, then the second-youngest gold medalist in history. In 1998, Kwan finished second to the youngest winner, Tara Lipinski, who immediately turned professional, at the age of 15. Kwan was just 17 herself at the time and has often said she feels old trying to fend off waves of young challengers.

But as she has remained in eligible ranks and matured, Kwan has also made women's skating mature along with her. It helped that after the premature losses of Baiul and Lipinski to the pros, the International Skating Union came up with new minimum-age requirements for Worlds. There are still young challengers, but fewer of them.

Choreography has become far more sophisticated and creative. And because prize money has made eligible ("amateur") skating financially rewarding, more top skaters have resisted the urge to turn professional. Thus, the same period that produced the ballistic youngsters also featured the oldest women's world champion ever. Maria Butyrskaya was 26 when she won at Helsinki in 1999.

"You notice that the women are taller and stronger, more fit and [more of them] have the complete package than before," said Canada's Jennifer Robinson who broke

into the top 10 for the first time in 2000 when she was 23. None of the first four that year were under 20.

Butyrskaya's championship was the first ever by a Russian woman and represented the climax of a long-term effort. For decades, Russia (when it was still the Soviet Union) did not produce notable women's singles skaters. The nation's best females were funneled into either pairs or dance. But by the mid-1990s, Russians were becoming as important a force in women's singles as Americans.

The top three women at Junior Worlds in 1998 and two of the top three in 1999 were Russians. Butyrskaya and Irina Slutskaya are the older, controlling force, but behind them a bunch of potential world medalists—Viktoria Volchkova, Elena Ivanova, Julia Soldatova, Daria Timoshenko among them—are building their arsenals.

The Kwan-Slutskaya duel of contrasting styles is a compelling one. "It's so hard because each of us [is] unique in our own way," says Kwan. "Irina's a really good person and you want her to do well and you want yourself to do well, and there's only one first place."

In the U.S., where the women's division is the one that matters most to the general public, there remains a bountiful harvest of contenders. Kwan is backed by the likes of Naomi Nari Nam, Sasha Cohen and 15-year-old world bronze medalist Sarah Hughes.

So, it should have come as no surprise that every one of the six berths in the final flight at 2001 Worlds was occupied by a Russian or American.

"You could see how much work we have to do," said seventh-place finisher Fumie Suguri of Japan.

But the work has already begun. Because most of the elite women are veteran competitors, even if they're young, performance levels have risen. At the 2001 Worlds, the number of "clean" programs in both the women's short and long programs ran far deeper into the field than ever before. Countries not traditionally strong in women's skating were making their mark: Italy's Silvia Fontana, Denmark's Mikkeline Kierkgaard, Uzbekistan's Tatiana Malinina.

And there are strong signs that, after a stagnant decade, the women are about to push the technical envelope again. It hasn't kept pace with the men's development. After Japan's Midori Ito landed a triple Axel at the 1992 Olympics, there hasn't been another one. But as many as six women were working on them for the 2002 Olympic season and there are a slew of new, difficult combination jumps, led by Slutskaya's triple/triple/double. The women will all be doing tougher elements for the same reason the men did: they'll have to in order to win.

And, combined with more competition-hardened fields, that can only be good for women's skating.

Michelle Kwan

Parting might be such sweet sorrow, but in this case Michelle Kwan was only too happy to say farewell.

"Goodbye, odd-year jinx! That's all I can say," Kwan grinned after she won the 2001 world championship in a skillful, passionate contest with rival Irina Slutskaya.

She was world champion in 1996, 1998 and 2000, but had finished "only" second in 1997 and 1999, prompting the flimsy criticism that she was hexed in the odd-numbered years. But when you've lived nearly a decade on the public stage, the spotlight shines brightly on every little aspect of your life.

Kwan was already well known in American skating circles by the time she came to the world's attention in 1994 as the most famous Olympic alternate in skating history. She was just 13 when she finished second at U.S. Nationals and was sent to the Lillehammer Olympics as a substitute in case Nancy Kerrigan—injured in the infamous incident involving Tonya Harding—couldn't skate. But Kerrigan was healthy enough to skate, and won a silver medal.

The attention from the Kerrigan-Harding circus helped groom Kwan for her starring roles in three of the most memorable duels in women's skating history.

In 1996, Kwan and Chen Lu of China each received two perfect 6.0s for their artistry, the only time that's ever happened in a women's freeskate at the world championship. Kwan, just 15, edged the refined defending champion for her first world title. Both women are known for their trademark elegance, gentle landings and flowing interpretation of music.

At the 1998 Nagano Winter Games, Kwan skated superbly enough to win any other Olympics. But in a 6-3 judging split, her 15-year-old American rival Tara Lipinski became the youngest Olympic champion ever. The gracious manner in which Kwan handled her emotionally devastating defeat inspired the audience at the world championships in Minneapolis to give her a standing ovation even before she skated.

- Michelle has written several books including *Michelle Kwan: Heart of a Champion* and *The Winning Attitude*, the first two in a series of eight. *People Magazine* chose her as one of the "50 Most Beautiful People in the World" in 2000.

Born July 7, 1980, Torrance, California
Hometown: Lake Arrowhead, California
Training Site: Lake Arrowhead
Coach: Frank Carroll
Choreographer: Lori Nichol

RESULTS

1996: 1st Worlds
1st U.S. Nationals

1997: 2nd Worlds
2nd U.S. Nationals

1998: 1st Worlds
2nd Olympics
1st U.S. Nationals

1999: 2nd Worlds
1st Skate America
1st Skate Canada
1st U.S. Nationals

2000: 1st Worlds
2nd Grand Prix Final
1st U.S. Nationals
1st Skate America

2001: 1st Worlds
2nd Grand Prix Final
1st U.S. Nationals

Champions on Ice | Detroit | May 2000

Worlds | Nice | March 2000
Classical yet modern, soft but also strong, Michelle is a blend of qualities that place her at the pinnacle of women's figure skating.

Skate Canada | Mississauga | November 2000

Worlds | Lausanne | March 1997

Winter Olympics | Nagano | February 1998

In 2001, there was the classic confrontation of styles between the exquisite Kwan, skating to "Song of the Black Swan," and the athletic Slutskaya, who landed the world's first triple/triple/double combination by a woman. The two good friends had been competing against each other since junior Worlds in 1994 and Slutskaya seemed to be surpassing Kwan, beating her in two head-to-head skates in the 2000–01 season. But Kwan attacked her program with fervor and her usual dignity and finished to a wild standing ovation, to become the first four-time American world champion since Peggy Fleming.

"When I finished the program and they were all on their feet, I just wanted to put it all in a little bottle and keep it forever," she said. "I've had a roller-coaster year and to end like this is truly amazing."

Just before the short program, Kwan's heel came loose from her boot. Rules say that if equipment isn't fixed by the time your name is called to skate, you're disqualified. Kwan's father Danny used "six screws and six tubes of super glue" to fix the skate and it was ready just in time.

Danny Kwan and his wife Estella came to California from Hong Kong in the early 1970s, and opened a restaurant in Torrance. They had three children: Ron, Karen and Michelle, the youngest. Michelle began skating at the age of five after watching Ron play hockey. Karen also skated and in 1995, they became the first sisters to compete against each other in senior Nationals in 36 years.

Champions on Ice | Detroit | February 1998

The Kwans are a close family and Michelle never competes without wearing a Chinese good luck charm around her neck. It was given to her by her grandmother.

"My grandmother, my grandfather, my parents, they're all hard workers," she says. "They have taught me so much. I think I'm very fortunate to have such a tight family...very supportive and loving. I think that's made a difference in my skating."

And Kwan has made a difference in skating. At 13, she became the youngest U.S. Olympic Festival champion ever, setting the tone for a future of record-breaking performances. The most stunning was the 1998 Nationals when she received 15 perfect marks for presentation, seven in the short program and eight in the freeskate.

By 1999, she was a 19-year-old freshman living in a dormitory at UCLA, still at the top of the skating world and trying to study on airplanes between competitions.

"I wanted the whole experience, the whole nine yards," she said about college. "When I was young, I didn't realize how lucky I was and now when I see the world and am in school studying and reading about things, it's amazing how those things can affect you."

At first, it was difficult to strike a balance between school and skating, and she struggled much of the season. But she peaked in time to win the 2000 Worlds after losing to Maria Butyrskaya the previous spring. She had become the first skater to reclaim the world title twice in her career.

'It just felt very satisfying to come back strong after so many people had said, 'Oh, she's over,' 'Oh, she's deteriorating,'" she said.

She's definitely not over. With four world titles, and an Olympic silver, all that remains is an Olympic title.

'I can say I'm a veteran at this now," Kwan says. "There's a lot of things I can take from Nagano. The Olympics won't be such a shock. I think I can go in there not expecting so much. I have all those medals now, so there are only things to gain."

Irina Slutskaya

When she was just a tot, whirling around the family's one-bedroom apartment in Moscow, her grandmother nicknamed her "The Typhoon."

Irina Slutskaya hasn't changed much since then.

She is still animated, still full of electricity and still chasing medals.

"When I was in competition for small children I would get flowers, dolls and congratulations," Slutskaya once said. "But I was always crying, 'I want a medal,'" She's got plenty of them, but not the one she really craves. Three times she has finished second at the world championship to her old friend and rival Michelle Kwan.

At the 2001 Worlds, Slutskaya and Kwan waged one of the best head-to-head battles of opposing styles in the history of the women's world championship. Skating right before Slutskaya, the American performed with determination, and a graceful passion while her Russian opponent followed with a program equally as passionate in its ferocious athleticism.

In the end, Kwan won seven of the nine judges, but Slutskaya won a world of respect for delivering a spectacular program, including the first triple/triple/double combination by a woman at Worlds. A stumble coming out of a difficult triple loop in combination with a triple Lutz may have been all that stood between Slutskaya and her first world title.

"I was pleased with everything," Slutskaya said afterward. "It was my best of the season. It was the judges' decision. It's just sport, and I'm just glad that I did well. I saw how well Michelle skated and it encouraged me to do well, too. I wanted to show my combinations, which are quite interesting."

Quite. No other woman has ever run off three jumps in combination. And in 2000 she became the first female to land triple Lutz/triple loop when she rode the combination to the gold medal at the Grand Prix Final. She also pioneered doing the Biellmann Spin first on one foot, then the other. That's the back-arching tulip-shaped spin in which the skater reaches back over her head to grab her skate. With all these innovations, Slutskaya has set a new technical standard which, combined with Kwan's artistry, is stirring the women's division out of its longtime doldrums.

"Michelle and I have been competing against each other for a long time now. We're good friends, but there can only be one first place," said Slutskaya, who had beaten

Born: February 9, 1979, Moscow

Hometown: Moscow

Training Site: Moscow

Coach: Zhanna Gromova

Choreographer: Elena Matveeva

RESULTS

1997: 4th Worlds
1st Europeans
3rd Russian Nationals

1998: 5th Olympics
2nd Worlds
2nd Europeans
4th Russian Nationals

1999: 1st Cup of Russia
3rd Grand Prix Final
4th Russian Nationals

2000: 2nd Worlds
1st Grand Prix Final
1st Europeans
1st NHK
1st Cup of Russia
1st Russian Nationals

2001: 2nd Worlds
1st Grand Prix Final
1st Europeans
1st Russian Nationals

Skate Canada | Mississauga
November 2000

• Irina's hobby is collecting stuffed animals, and she has over 200 of them.

Skate Canada | Mississauga | November 2000

Skate Canada | Mississauga | November 2000
Dynamic and artistic, Irina commands attention the moment she steps onto the ice.

Kwan twice earlier in the 2001 season. "And I think we've learned from each other."

Slutskaya has certainly learned to be as engaging on the ice as she has always been off it. She burst onto the world scene as an energetic 15-year-old jumper, finishing third to Kwan at the 1994 Junior Worlds, which she won the next season. In 1996, she became the first Russian woman to win the European title, and when she repeated in 1997, it completed Russia's sweep of all four golds, the first time one country had captured all four European titles.

But, despite her successes, she always skated with an isolated determination, seeming to concentrate more on her jumps than on the audience. That began to change,

though, with a skating disaster: her triple Lutz inexplicably deserted her during the 1998–99 season. After finishing second at the '98 Worlds she could not even make the Russian team for Europeans or Worlds the following year, and considered retiring from the sport.

"It was a shock. I never thought I would drop so fast," she admitted. "I couldn't go five minutes on the ice without crying. I couldn't even watch Worlds on TV."

But, in her misery, Slutskaya discovered how much she loved figure skating, and resumed training with a new energy. She worked on toning her body, paid more attention to the little details of skating, became more fluent in English, switched to choreographer Elena Matveeva, chose more mature programs and, she says, "just grew

Skate Canada | Mississauga | November 2000

up." She also married her boyfriend, Sergei Mikheyev, on August 6, 1999.

Her new happiness and emotional stability was reflected in her skating, and during the 1999–2000 season, she won her first National title, her third European crown, the Grand Prix Final and was second at Worlds. The stunning comeback set the stage for a renewal of her rivalry with Kwan, which will probably culminate at the 2002 Salt Lake City Olympics.

But her dogged recovery from the despair of 1998 did not surprise those people who knew her best. When she was just four, Slutskaya's mother, Natalia, a teacher and a talented skier in her youth, introduced her daughter to skating at one of Moscow's outdoor rinks because she thought the fresh air would be good for her. Soon, she started to train with Zhanna Gromova, still the only coach she has ever had.

Gromova recalls the Slutskaya of those early years as "a tiny butterball of energy, all bundled up in layers of clothes, always smiling, always ready to go, always trying." That description could apply almost word-for-word today.

"I want to come back with something new," she says of the 2002 Olympics. "I have to take my heart into my hands and encourage myself to go on."

She always does.

Sarah Hughes

Sarah Hughes figures that success does not come to the timid.

"You've got to grab for it," Hughes said in March 2001, after she won a world bronze medal at the age of 15. "You can't just be safe. You have to tell everyone you want it."

Hughes practices what she preaches. When she was three years old, she learned to tie her own skate laces so she didn't have to wait for her mother, Amy, to finish with her older children's skates. At five, Sarah could land double toe loops and double Salchows.

When she was six, Hughes wowed a full house with her poise in an ice show at Lake Placid, headlined by Kristi Yamaguchi. At eight, she toured France and Switzerland with world champion ice dancers Maia Usova and Sasha Zhulin. She worked with coach Jeff DiGregorio, a jumping specialist, then moved to Robin Wagner and trained in Hackensack, New Jersey. Before her 13th birthday, Hughes had mastered all five triple jumps used by elite women skaters, and claimed the U.S. Junior championship.

The next year, when she was still 13, she won a silver medal at Junior Worlds and finished fourth at U.S. senior Nationals. It was a stunning achievement but a spot short of a berth on the 1999 World team. But second-place finisher Naomi Nari Nam was even younger than Hughes and the International Skating Union had a rule prohibiting any skater under 15, unless she had won a world junior medal. So Hughes went to Worlds, her first senior international of any kind. She finished an unexpected seventh, and she wasn't even in high school yet!

Hughes was earning a reputation for pushing the technical envelope. She was doing the triple Salchow/triple loop combinations and was also working on the extremely rare triple loop/triple loop and was practicing triple Axels.

Wagner gave her a more mature freeskate program, Don Quixote, for the 2000–01 season and Hughes' increased sophistication was immediately evident. She made the podium in all three of her Grand Prix events, finished second at the U.S. Nationals, third at the Grand Prix Final and third at Vancouver, for her first Worlds medal.

"I worked really hard for it," understated the self-motivated Hughes. "It's been a dream season."

Born: May 2, 1935, Great Neck, N.Y.

Hometown: Great Neck, N.Y.

Training Site: Great Neck, N.Y.

Coach: Robin Wagner

Choreographer: Robin Wagner

RESULTS

1999: 7th Worlds
2nd World Juniors
4th Skate America
3rd Trophée Lalique
1st Vienna Cup
4th U.S. Nationals

2000: 5th Worlds
2nd Sparkassen Cup
2nd Skate America
3rd Cup of Russia
3rd U.S. Nationals

2001: 3rd Worlds
2nd U.S. Nationals

- When she won her bronze at 2001 Worlds, Sarah was still just a sophomore at Great Neck High School, doing her homework in the car on the long drive to the rink.

Worlds | Vancouver | March 2001

Worlds | Vancouver | March 2001
Sarah's great form is matched by great interpretation and delivery.

Angela Nikodinov

The turning point in Angela Nikodinov's career occurred off the ice and had nothing to do with figure skating.

In the summer of 2000, Nikodinov was in Salt Lake City attending an Olympic seminar. Speed-skating great Dan Jansen stood up to address the collection of athletes. He told of his life's challenges and of winning an Olympic gold medal in his final race.

"He's been one of my heroes forever," Nikodinov recalled. "Just listening to him tell his story, I was crying because it brought out all the emotions I've felt the past two years."

Jansen's speech inspired Nikodinov to set higher goals and have the best year of her skating career. She won her second medal at U.S. Nationals. She also finished third in the short program at Worlds, and fifth overall, a leap of four places in a year when everyone was skating well.

"I feel like a totally different skater," Nikodinov said. "I don't even compare my skating this year to last."

Nikodinov said that until the 2000–01 season, she had often fought herself and that, "a lack of confidence has held me back." Indeed, even when she was eighth at U.S. Nationals at the age of 15, her longtime choreographer Elena Tcherkasskaya often had to remind her to smile during her programs.

Nikodinov is the only child of Bulgarian immigrants, Nick and Dolores, and she is fluent in both English and her parents' native tongue. She began skating at a small rink near her California home when she was five years old. At nine, she started skating with veteran coach John Nicks, and stayed with him until she was 16, when she switched to Lake Arrowhead and Peter Oppegard.

Although she would often be tentative in competitions, by 1997 Nikodinov had moved into the top five in the U.S. In 1999 she won her first medal, a bronze, and a berth on the American team for Worlds. Just two weeks before Worlds, she left California to train in Michigan with Richard Callaghan.

In 2000 she qualified for Worlds because silver medalist Sasha Cohen was too young. Nikodinov made the most of her opportunity, winning Four Continents and finishing ninth at Worlds.

She had gained self-confidence and, after hearing Jansen, a sense of purpose. Early in the 2000–01 season, she returned to California. Tcherkasskaya became her coach. She received a heartfelt standing ovation at U.S. Nationals and skated superbly at Worlds. But more importantly, she liked the way she performed.

Born: May 9, 1980,
Spartanburg, South Carolina

Hometown: San Pedro, California

Training Site: Lake Arrowhead, California

Coach: Elena Tcherkasskaya

Choreographer: Elena Tcherkasskaya

RESULTS

1999: 12th Worlds
3rd Four Continents
3rd U.S. Nationals

2000: 9th Worlds
1st Four Continents
5th Skate America
4th NHK
4th U.S. Nationals

2001: 5th Worlds
2nd Four Continents
3rd U.S. Nationals

- During 1999 U.S. Nationals Tara Lipinski called from the Stars on Ice tour to give Angela a pep talk.

Four Continents | Salt Lake City
February 2001

Four Continents | Salt Lake City
February 2001

Maria Butyrskaya

Maria Butyrskaya was 15 when her coach at Moscow's Central Army Club told her to get out of the sport.

"She said I was not a figure skater, I had no talent," Butyrskaya recalls with a quick, but pained, smile. "She said that I must finish."

It may have taken a while, but Butyrskaya proved that coach, and all her doubters, wrong. Very wrong. In 1999 she became, at the age of 26, the first Russian woman to win the world championship. Along the way, Butyrskaya had to overcome severe political and social upheaval, difficult economic times and her own destructive nervousness.

"Well, I'm still all the time nervous when I skate," she laughs. "There's been no change in that."

When she subdues that tenseness, her maturity and elegance usually put her on the podium. And she is very close to conquering the triple Axel, a jump which hasn't been landed in eligible competition by a woman since the 1994 Olympics.

Nothing has come easily for Butyrskaya. After the Soviet Union fell apart in the early 1990s, there was little money for skating, and it was a four-hour round trip from her apartment to the training rink. She finished fourth at Europeans in 1994, but was somehow kept out of the Olympics. And in late 1999, her car was destroyed by a bomb. "They never found out who did it, or why," she says.

Butyrskaya's parents, both engineers, enrolled her in skating when she was four. She won every local competition and was soon accepted into the prestigious Central Army Club. Her big breakthrough came with a bronze medal at the 1995 Europeans. She won the 1998 and '99 European titles under coach Elena Tchaikovskaya. In 1999, at Helsinki, she became world champion.

At the end of the 1990s, the decade when Michelle Kwan and Oksana Baiul had won Worlds at 15 years of age and Tara Lipinski at 14, Maria Butyrskaya had tri-umphed at 26. She is the oldest women's world champion in history, a fact in which she is justifiably proud.

"I am not afraid of the young girls," she says. "For me, age doesn't matter. I like to skate and I like to compete. I think it is good for everyone, even the younger ones. They can look at me and say, 'If Maria can stay in and do it, then so can I.'"

Born: June 28, 1972, Moscow

Hometown: Moscow

Training Site: Moscow

Coaches: Elena Tchaikovskaya, Vladimir Kotin

Choreographer: Elena Tchaikovskaya

RESULTS

1996: 4th Worlds
3rd Europeans
1st Russian Nationals

1997: 5th Worlds
4th Europeans
1st Russian Nationals

1998: 4th Olympics
3rd Worlds
1st Europeans
1st Russian Nationals

1999: 1st Worlds
3rd Grand Prix Final
1st Europeans
1st Cup of Russia

3rd Sparkassen Cup
1st Russian Nationals

2000: 3rd Worlds
1st Grand Prix Final
2nd Europeans
1st Trophee Lalique
2nd NHK
1st Sparkassen Cup
2nd Russian Nationals

2001: 2nd Europeans
4th Grand Prix Final
3rd Russian Nationals

- Maria may move to the U.S. for a pro career but says, "I love living in Russia. My coach is here. I love my apartment and I live only 20 minutes from my parents' place."

Winter Olympics | Nagano | February 1998

Fumie Suguri

At an age when most elite athletes are already competing internationally, Fumie Suguri had not even started skating seriously.

"I spent a lot of time with skating just as a hobby," says the 2001 Four Continents champion. "I didn't start real training, like an athlete, until I was nearly 15 years old."

But once she dedicated herself to the sport, it took her only two years to win her first Japanese championship.

In the Suguri family, the skating of Fumie and her younger sister Chika always took a back seat to the demands of a good education. Suguri went to a private high school in Yokohama, where expectations were high and homework was heavy, so she had time for only limited training. But when she finished 11th at Junior Nationals in 1995, Suguri was disappointed. She increased her training time to three hours per day, somehow found the time to prepare for the difficult Japanese university entrance exams, and within a year was able to land all five triples. She also hired Canada's Lori Nichol, Michelle Kwan's choreographer, and the two have worked together ever since.

Although she showed plenty of promise, Suguri's career sputtered after her first national title in 1997.

"I went to Nagano just to watch [the Olympics]," she recalls. "I didn't really feel good, but it was a good experience to learn just how disappointed I was [in not making the team], and not let that happen again."

After some switching of coaches and a 20th place finish without a coach at the 1999 Worlds, in 2000 Suguri turned to highly regarded Nobuo Sato, father and coach of 1994 world champion Yuka Sato, but she was plagued by injuries to both ankles and missed the world team again. But the 2000–01 season demonstrated what a healthy Suguri can do. She finished third at Skate Canada, her first international medal in two years, then won the Four Continents.

At 2001 Worlds, she delivered a stunning, but undermarked, short program. She finished seventh overall, an extraordinary rise of 13 places in two years. But she isn't satisfied.

"I'm not really proud of myself because I have my own goals and want to go higher," she said. "I guess it doesn't happen right away."

Especially with such a late start.

Born: December 31, 1980, Chiba.

Hometown: Yokohama

Training site: Yokohama

Coach: Nobuo Sato

Choreographer: Lori Nichol

RESULTS

1998: 3rd NHK

1999: 20th Worlds
5th Grand Prix Final
7th Trophee Lalique
5th Four Continents

2000: 4th Four Continents
3rd Skate Canada
3rd NHK

2001: 7th Worlds
1st Four Continents

- Fumie's father is an airline pilot and moved the family to Alaska for two years when Fumie was three. Her mother took her to the skating rink in Yokohama at age six, because she wanted "my body to remember all the good outdoor things we did in Alaska."

Four Continents | Salt Lake City | February 2001

Four Continents | Salt Lake City February 2001

Four Continents | Salt Lake City February 2001

Four Continents | Salt Lake City | February 2001
Perhaps Fumie's greatest asset is her gracefulness.

Vanessa Gusmeroli

It appears that to win the French women's figure skating championship, you must be a world-class competitor in another sport as well.

Surya Bonaly was French champion, and world silver medalist, during the 1990s, but she first gained international recognition as European junior champion on the trampoline. Vanessa Gusmeroli has won the last two French Nationals, and a bronze medal at the 1997 Worlds, but she feels equally at home on ice or on water that hasn't been frozen. Gusmeroli is an accomplished water-skier, winning the French junior championship and finishing second at the 1991 European Championships.

Gusmeroli began figure skating when she was six, but that seems positively ancient compared to her introduction to water-skiing, which came at the age of two. She would spend summers behind a boat on Lake Annecy, and winters behind a Zamboni at the Annecy Figure Skating Club.

Gusmeroli began to draw attention when she finished fourth at Junior Worlds in 1994. She made her world championship debut in 1996 at Edmonton. She finished 14th but impressed fans with her huge jumps and her use of "hydro-blading," which requires tremendous balance and leg strength.

Although she showed great potential, her bronze medal at the 1997 Worlds caught most people, even Gusmeroli herself, by surprise. Only Tara Lipinski and Michelle Kwan beat her.

"I was intimidated in the warm-up," she said, but then skated one of the best performances of her life, recovering from an early fall to land five triples and seize her unexpected spot on the podium.

"I was very grateful to be finally acknowledged by the skating community. It meant so much to me to win this medal," she said afterward, but she also wondered if staying anonymous might have been easier. She sometimes gets so nervous that it really affects her skating.

Conquering those nerves, and successfully landing her enormous triples more regularly, are all that stands between Gusmeroli and consistently high international placings. She has the physical talent, and usually reaps high marks for her mature presentations, but her results are mercurial. She was a promising sixth at the 1998 Olympics,

Born: September 19, 1978, Annecy

Hometown: Annecy

Training Site: Paris

Coaches: Katia Beyer, Stanislav Leonovich

Choreographer: Sandra Garde

RESULTS

1997: 3rd Worlds

1998: 16th Worlds
6th Olympics

1999: 5th Worlds
5th Europeans
2nd Sparkassen Cup

2000: 5th Grand Prix Final
4th Worlds
4th Europeans
4th Sparkassen Cup

2001: 9th Worlds
4th Europeans

- Vanessa's parents ran a pizzeria in La Clusaz, where she tried ice dancing, but preferred the jumps of singles skating.

Winter Olympics | Nagano | February 1998

for instance, but struggled at the Worlds just five weeks later and finished 16th.

Gusmeroli moved to Paris in the middle of the 1999–2000 season to work with Stanislav Leonovich and Katia Beyer. She left behind the only coach she'd ever had, Didier Lucine, and her familiar life in Annecy, as part of a makeover designed to help her reach the podium at the 2002 Olympics. Those close to the French skating scene say they're seeing a far more serene and confident Vanessa Gusmeroli.

◀ Worlds | Minneapolis | March 1998
Great moves, great speed and great programs help Vanessa's campaign for a medal for France.

Elena Liashenko

I f it's difficult for skating fans to understand why some skaters aren't consistent, it's often more difficult for the skaters themselves to figure out.

Elena Liashenko has had competitive results which look like a snakes-and-ladders game board. In 1994, when the Ukraine native was 17, she finished 19th in her first European championships and 19th again at the Lillehammer Olympics. Yet a month later, she was sixth at Worlds! And two years later, she was back down to 12th in the world, missed the Worlds entirely a year later, then came back to finish seventh the year after that.

But by the 1998–99 season, Liashenko was a top-five skater at Europeans and a solid top-10 finisher at Worlds. Despite starting the season with a serious groin injury, she won her first Grand Prix event, with a shocking gold at Skate Canada '98 in Kamloops, B.C. She also made her first Grand Prix Final, "which was really my most important goal of the year," she said. The next season, she was the only woman not from Russia or the U.S. to qualify for the Grand Prix Final.

"I can't explain it," she said of her improvement. "It just happened by itself. Maybe it's because I am drawing more pleasure from skating. I feel inspired inside When I was younger, it was much harder for me. Now I understand more and strive toward a goal."

Liashenko grew up in Kiev, and began skating when she was four, but the Dinko rink in Kiev where she trained was not the best atmosphere for elite skating. There was no heat, no ice-resurfacing machine and Liashenko was forced to spend four hours a day commuting from home to the rink. When she transferred to the new arena in Kiev in the late 1990s, things improved dramatically.

Liashenko has graduated from the Kiev University of Culture and Sports and works as a sports instructor. And now that she's stabilized herself as a top-eight contender, she wants to take the next step.

"I understand that it will be difficult," she told a skating magazine, "but I believe I can compete for, if not the top spot at Worlds, then, at least a medal. If it doesn't happen this year, then, there's next year."

- Elena's hobbies are reading, knitting and visiting friends She says she can't remember a time when she didn't skate.

Winter Olympics | Nagano | February 1998
Elena shows athleticism and artistry.

Born: August 9, 1976, Kiev, Ukraine

Hometown: Kiev

Training Site: Kiev

Coach: Marina Amirkhanova

Choreographer: Irina Chubarets

RESULTS

1999: 8th Worlds
7th Europeans
6th Grand Prix Final
1st Nebelhorn Trophy
2nd Sparkassen Cup
4th NHK

2000: 10th Worlds
5th Europeans
5th Grand Prix Final
4th Sparkassen Cup
6th Cup of Russia

2001: 8th Worlds
4th Europeans

Winter Olympics | Nagano
February 1998

Silvia Fontana

Very few 10th-place finishes have ever been celebrated with such unbridled joy.

"I just cried and cried," said Italy's Silvia Fontana, after she finally made the top 10 at 2001 Worlds, when she was 24 years old.

"I couldn't contain it, which is strange because in every day life I'm pretty calm. It was a long journey to get there."

It had been more than 25 years since an Italian woman finished in the top 10. Quite an achievement for a woman who spent the first 10 years of her career skating "in a rink the size of a room."

Fontana was born in New York City, of Italian parents. Her father, an engineering contractor, was in the U.S. to construct a building he had designed, and when Fontana was six years old the family returned to Rome. There her father built a sports center, with a swimming pool, a gymnasium and a narrow ice rink, just 19 meters long.

"My mother would just park me there. We could do all kinds of sports, but I really loved the skating. It was the only rink in Rome until I was 13, so I got a very late start skating competitively. Even though I'd been to Worlds a couple of times, when I was 19, I could still do only two triples. I learned them all that year."

That was the year after she had moved back to the U.S. to train at Lake Arrowhead, California. In 1999, she moved from California to Simsbury, Connecticut, mainly to be with her longtime boyfriend, U.S. pairs skater John Zimmerman. She also wanted to work with Galina Zmievskaya, who had coached Victor Petrenko to an Olympic gold.

"I loved her intensity and passion and that's what I needed, someone who would go for every little detail and polish," Fontana says.

In Vancouver, she was well prepared psychologically and physically, and finished 10th, nine spots better than the previous year.

"Everyone was shocked...including me," she said of her emotional reaction. "It is a feeling that there is no price for."

- Silvia speaks Italian, French, English, German and Spanish. She is taking courses, long distance, for her Doctorate in Sociology at an Italian University. Her professors "don't even know I live in the U.S. or that I'm a skater."

Born: December 3, 1976, New York City

Hometown: Rome

Training Site: Simsbury, Connecticut

Coach: Galina Zmievskaya

Choreographer: Nina Petrenko

RESULTS

1999: 16th Worlds
13th Europeans
5th Skate Canada
9th Cup of Russia
1st Italian Nationals

2000: 19th Worlds
8th Europeans
10th Trophee Lalique
9th Cup of Russia
1st Italian Nationals

2001: 10th Worlds
11th Europeans
2nd Italian Nationals

Worlds | Vancouver
March 2001

Worlds | Helsinki | March 1999

◀ Skate Canada | St. John | November 1999
Superb presentation and unique emotion are part of Silvia's skating.

Jennifer Robinson

Jennifer Robinson knows that the only way to handle being thrown from a horse is to hop back in the saddle. So, her tumble from the world's top-10 ranking gave her motivation, not misery.

"I'm very disappointed, for sure, at the way the season ended," she said after finishing 15th at the 2001 Worlds, down seven spots from the year before. "But I'll be right back out there next week, starting on next year's programs."

Robinson is no stranger to recovering from setbacks. After qualifying for two world championships and winning the 1996 Canadian title, she suffered through two dismal Nationals in succession, missing the world team in both 1997 and 1998.

After 1998 Nationals, Robinson's coaches Doug and Michelle Leigh suggested she spend the summer training with Richard Callaghan in Detroit, just across the border from her parents' home in Windsor. She hadn't lived at home in seven years, since she moved to the Leighs' Mariposa School in Barrie, Ontario, and the experience agreed with her. Robinson also hired choreographer Lori Nichol, who designed programs which accentuated her elegant lines and graceful style. "I'm considered tall for a skater," the 5'8" Robinson says. "Lori uses that."

By January, she had reclaimed her Canadian championship and went on to win again in 2000 and 2001, the first time in 17 years that a woman had captured three straight national titles. More importantly, she won her first international medals with a bronze at Skate Canada and a silver at the Canadian Open in 1999, and then shocked even herself with her breakthrough performance at the 2000 Worlds.

Robinson's biggest problem in competition had been being overly cautious and landing her triples on two feet. But while doing housework two weeks before the 2000 Worlds, she cut her foot on a piece of glass. "Ironically, it

Born: December 2, 1976, Goderich, Ontario

Hometown: Windsor, Ontario

Training Site: Barrie, Ontario

Coaches: Michelle Leigh, Doug Leigh

Choreographer: Lori Nichol

RESULTS

1999: 18th Worlds
7th Four Continents
1st Canadian Nationals

5th Trophee Lalique
1st Canadian Nationals

2000: 8th Worlds
6th Four Continents
4th Skate Canada

2001: 15th Worlds
8th Four Continents
1st Canadian Nationals

- Robinson's brother, Jason, plays professional hockey and her uncle, Gaston Gingras, won a Stanley Cup with the 1986 champion Montreal Canadiens.

◀ Worlds | Nice | March 2000

hurt more whenever I two-footed my jumps. So I started doing clean programs...everything on one foot!"

Her top-10 finish meant that Canada could send two women to the next Worlds for the first time in six years.

Robinson increased her overall speed noticeably in 2001. "You've got to keep on working and improving," she says. It's the only way to climb back on the horse.

Skate Canada | Mississauga
November 2000

Skate Canada | Mississauga
November 2000

◀ Skate Canada | Mississauga | November 2000
Classic moves go with Jennifer's classic beauty.

Mikkeline Kierkgaard

In recent years, when a skater has arrived on the world scene with a splash, the ripples have usually been caused by jumping ability. But Mikkeline Kierkgaard has made big waves because of her artistry. She is still perfecting the triple Lutz, but she glides across the ice and performs with what every expert calls a style "beyond her years."

"She is the most talented Danish skater ever," adds Ingelise Blangsted, chairman of the Danish Skating Union.

When she was just 15, Kierkgaard moved into senior ranks and won the Danish Championship. That put her into the European Championships where her surprising seventh-place finish was the highest ever by a Danish woman in a major ISU event.

Kierkgaard is one of the youngest skaters on the world scene but she is the oldest of seven children in her family. She put on her first pair of skates at the age of three, and began competing when she was eight. From there, she made rapid progress. When she was 11, she and her coach Henrik Walentin began spending summers in California training with coach Frank Carroll and his star student Michelle Kwan, Kierkgaard's idol.

The summer training paid off as she won the Nordic Junior championships in 1998, when she was just 13, then won again the next year. But her European and World debuts in 2000 put her in a new class. A few weeks after her seventh-place finish at Europeans, she stunned the skating community with a second-place finish in her qualifying group at Worlds, behind Maria Butyrskaya. Kierkgaard's nerves got the better of her and she missed her combination in the short program, but she rebounded to finish 11th overall in her first Worlds.

"I did better than I could ever expect and I was very satisfied that I skated almost clean in the long program," she said. "I have a lot of years to go. I know what it takes now."

Movie producers have noticed Kierkgaard's magnetic presence and in the summer of 2001 she performed the skating scenes for actress Claire Danes' lead role in a movie called *It's All About Love*.

For Kierkgaard it's all about performing.

Born: May 25, 1984, Hundested, Denmark

Hometown: Humelbaek

Training Site: Horsholm

Coach: Henrik Walentin

Choreographer: Henrik Walentin

RESULTS

1999: 13th Junior Worlds
1st Nordic Juniors
3rd Salchow Trophy

2000: 11th Worlds
7th Europeans
12th Junior Worlds

2001: 14th Worlds
1st Nordic Seniors

- When she was 10, Mikkeline had a chance to join the World Ballet School of Denmark, but chose to remain in skating instead.

Worlds | Vancouver
March 2001

Worlds | Nice | March 2000
Mikkeline's trademarks: long glides and gorgeous edges.

Viktoria Volchkova

The power of radio is responsible for creating one of the bright young stars in the constellation of promising Russian skaters.

Viktoria Volchkova's parents heard a radio announcement about figure skating lessons and took their six-year-old daughter to a rink in St. Petersburg (then Leningrad). Volchkova showed an aptitude for jumping, and because of the fertile history of pairs at the famous Yubileny Rink, she wanted to skate pairs. But she was considered too tall and was put in singles, which was also agreeable because her idol was Oksana Baiul, the 1994 Olympic singles champion.

Eventually Volchkova moved to Moscow to train with Viktor Kudriavtsev, who would help her work her way through the extraordinarily competitive women's ranks in Russia. At 16 she finished third at Junior Worlds, behind two other Russian juniors! And with Maria Butyrskaya and Irina Slutskaya both still on the scene, it was becoming very crowded at the top of the Russian women's pyramid.

"Russian Nationals are like a minefield," says Volchkova. "There is a lot of pressure; any mistake can be fatal."

Volchkova won the Junior Grand Prix Final in 1999 and also qualified for her first Europeans and Worlds by finishing third at Russian senior Nationals. She went on to win her first of three straight European bronze medals.

"When I won that medal at Europeans, I knew all that work I was doing for years really paid off and that I'm on the right track," she said.

Volchkova finished a credible 10th in her world championship debut in 1999, and moved up to sixth for the next two years.

She is studying at the Institute for Physical Culture, and is considering a future career in journalism. Perhaps one day it will be her voice on radio, inspiring parents to register their young children in figure skating.

Born: July 30, 1982, Leningrad

Hometown: St. Petersburg

Training Site: Moscow

Coaches: Viktor Kudriavtsev, Igor Rusakov

Choreographer: K. Kudrin

RESULTS

1998: 3rd World Juniors
5th Russian Nationals

1999: 10th Worlds
3rd Europeans
3rd World Juniors
3rd Goodwill Games
2nd Trophee Lalique
2nd NHK
3rd Russian Nationals

2000: 6th Worlds
3rd Europeans
6th Grand Prix Final
4th Skate America
5th Cup of Russia
2nd Trophee Lalique
3rd Russian Nationals

2001: 6th Worlds
3rd Europeans
2nd Russian Nationals

Worlds | Vancouver | March 2001

• Viktoria added a second coach, Igor Rusakov, in 2000 to add variety to her training.

Worlds | Vancouver | March 2001
A long stretch looks beautiful on a tall skater like Viktoria.

Tatiana Malinina

The figure skating career of Tatiana Malinina has been one long roller-coaster ride, but she doesn't want to get off.

"I didn't stop because I love figure skating and I can't imagine a life without it," she said of her choice to remain eligible after the 1998 season, when she was already 25 years old and had finished an obscure 14th at Worlds.

Her perseverance was rewarded with a spectacular 1998–99 season when she won her first-ever international medals, with a gold at NHK and a stunning first-place finish in the Grand Prix Final.

And when the 1999 Worlds rolled around, just a year after people had wondered aloud why she was still skating, she missed the podium by just one spot, finishing fourth. A few months later, she won the inaugural Four Continents Championship.

With her solid jumps and spins, Malinina continued to medal at Grand Prix events, although her world championship results slipped dramatically over the next couple of years, mostly because of injuries and costly errors in the short program. But Malinina knows she can battle back because she's done it before.

Malinina grew up in Novosibirsk, amid the dramatic climate of Siberia. Her father is a former figure skater, who served as her coach for 18 years, and her mother is a former gymnast. When Malinina was a teenager, the family moved to the Uzbekistan capital of Tashkent, an ancient city on the fabled spice route to the Orient.

When the Soviet Union broke up in 1991, Malinina chose to compete for Uzbekistan. But when their training rink closed in 1996, she and her boyfriend, fellow Uzbekistan skater Roman Skorniakov, decided to leave the country. After a stop in Russia, they ended up in Dale City, Virginia, in late 1998. Malinina and Skorniakov act as each other's coach, and in January 2000, they also became husband and wife.

Her victories at the Grand Prix Final and Four Continents were the first medals ever won by Uzbekistan. And she was 26 when she won them.

"Everyone thinks she is too old to compete," says her husband. "But she thinks she is 16 and is skating like she's 16."

🔺 Skate America | Detroit | October 1998
Tatiana uses her hands to great effect.

Born: January 28, 1973, Novosibirsk, Russia

Hometown: Tashkent, Uzbekistan

Training Site: Dale City, Virginia

Coach: None

Choreographer: Rostislav Sinitsyn

RESULTS

1998: 8th Olympics
14th Worlds
1st Skate Israel

1999: 4th Worlds
1st Grand Prix Final
1st Four Continents
1st Asian Games
3rd NHK

2000: 18th Worlds
7th Four Continents
3rd Sparkassen Cup
3rd NHK

2001: 13th Worlds
4th Four Continents
5th Grand Prix Final

• Before devoting herself to skating Tatiana studied gymnastics, ballroom dancing and swimming.

Four Continents | Salt Lake City | February 2001

Annie Bellemare

If what doesn't kill us makes us stronger, Annie Bellemare came out of the 2001 season more powerful than she went in.

Bellemare qualified for her first world championship, finishing 21st, but along the way survived injury scares, a sudden-death skate-off at Four Continents for the final berth on the Canadian world team, and nearly missing the cut in the qualifying rounds.

The most frightening incident came at Patinage Plus, a skating boutique she and her mother run in suburban Montreal. Two weeks before her world championship debut—a moment for which she'd waited 15 years—a 500-pound stack of wood toppled onto her right foot.

"It felt like it was broken and I thought, 'Oh no, I can't go to Worlds,'" she said. But x-rays were negative and she was back on the ice in a couple of days. She made it to Worlds, where she encountered another huge pile—of pressure. After struggling in the qualifying round, she settled down and landed a world-class triple Lutz/double toe loop in the short program and finished 21st overall.

"I learned a lot I can use, about handling myself at a world championship," she said later, and hopes to put that experience to work by remaining eligible until the 2006 Olympics, "where I plan to win a medal."

If she does, she'll fulfull a vow she made at the age of eight, after watching Liz Manley on TV, biting her silver medal in 1988. "I told my neighbor I was going to win one too," she recalls.

If she adds consistency to her jumps, and continues to work on her artistry, she has the potential to do just that.

⚜ Worlds | Vancouver | March 2001
Annie performs classic skating stances to perfection.

Born: January 2, 1980, Laval, Quebec

Hometown: St. Eustache

Training Site: Boucherville

Coach: Stephane Yvars

Choreographers: Julie Brault, Marijane Stong

RESULTS

2000: 3rd Four Continents
9th Skate Canada
10th Cup of Russia
3rd Canadian Nationals

2001: 21st Worlds
9th Four Continents
3rd Canadian Nationals

• Annie says the turning point in her career was winning a silver at 1999 Nationals. "Everything got so big from there," she said.

Worlds | Vancouver | March 2001

THE
PAIRS
TEAMS

Jamie Sale and David Pelletier

Elena Berezhnaya and Anton Sikharulidze

Xue Shen and Hongbo Zhao

Maria Petrova and Alexei Tikhonov

Kyoko Ina and John Zimmerman

Kristy Wirtz and Kris Wirtz

Tatiana Totmianina and Maxim Marinin

Dorota Zagorska and Mariusz Siudek

Tiffany Scott and Philip Dulebohn

Sarah Abitbol and Stephane Bernadis

Just when it appeared that there was a serious decline in pairs interest around the world, there has been a sudden revival.

The three countries with the most skating depth—Canada, Russia and the U.S.—are still the driving forces in pairs. But other countries, particularly China, are discovering, and mastering, the discipline. Inspired by three-time world medalists Xue Shen and Hongbo Zhao, the Chinese are taking pairs so seriously that they provided the top five finishers in the pairs event at the 2001 Junior Grand Prix Finals.

In France, a long-dormant pairs interest has been reawakened by the 2000 World bronze won by Sarah Abitbol and Stephane Bernadis. There were a record five pairs entries in the 2001 French Nationals.

And at the world championships from 1998–2001, seven different countries were represented on the pairs podium. Heading into the Salt Lake City Olympics, there were six active pairs who'd won world medals.

All that said, elite pairs is still a Russian-dominated event. When Canadians Jamie Sale and David Pelletier skated lyrically to their first world title in 2001, it was just the seventh time in 37 years that a Russian pair had not won Worlds. But in recent years, it is no longer automatic that a Russian pair will win. By the turn of the century a brilliant three-way rivalry had developed among the Canadians, the Chinese and twice-champion Russian pair Elena Berezhnaya and Anton Sikharulidze. While the Russians always had the potential to be one

of the best pairs of all time, they rarely skated that way in competition until pressed by their new rivals.

"It's more pressure, but at the same time it's more pressure for us to skate better, to be stronger, and we feel like fighting," says Sikharulidze. "I think in this kind of situation, nobody can win all competitions. Everybody, maybe three or four pairs, are too close, and it's really, really high level."

The second level of teams, all with a chance at the podium, have also improved steadily, so that the freeskate final at 2001 Worlds was regarded as one of the best, and deepest, nights of pairs skating in history.

The concept of pairs skating took a right-angle turn before the 2000–01 season, mainly because Sale and Pelletier's successful world debut had brought a new equation to the game. There have been various stages of pairs skating over the past quarter-century, shifting from an emphasis on side-by-side jumps in the early 1980s, to huge throws and complex lifts.

"Often the guy was the stem and the girl was the flower," is the way Canadian choreographer Lori Nichol described the standard pairs skating look.

But Sale and Pelletier brought a musical unison, intense inter-partner chemistry and a dance-like choreography with their breakthrough Love Story program in 2000. By the next season, all the top pairs were trying to tell a story through choreography and were trying to connect more noticeably with each other on the ice.

It is harder to bring that seamless, emotional choreography to pairs than to any other discipline. Essentially, pairs skating is free skating performed in unison. The partners' movements are supposed to be synchronized whether they are together or apart. But because the man must be big enough to throw his partner great distances, and the woman must be small enough to be aerodynamic, it's difficult to get the right physical match so that their lines are in harmony. And when one partner is trying complicated tasks while duplicating, or mirroring, the exact movements of the other, it's often too much to demand that they also connect with passion. But that's what the top pairs must now do.

There is also a huge fear factor. There is no job in figure skating, and few in any sport, more dangerous than being a pairs skater. The woman must be courageous because she is being propelled for distances as far as 20 feet, or held aloft by one hand of a partner who is doing turns. The man is constantly in danger of his head and face being sliced during the extremely complicated new dismounts from lifts.

So pairs skaters must be of the right build, technically accomplished enough to land triple jumps—some couples are doing two different ones—brave enough to handle the potential for serious injury, trained well enough to match their partner's movements, and calm and passionate enough to demonstrate an emotional connection.

With so many complex requirements it's no wonder many countries simply can't find enough skaters to build a strong pairs program. And it's no wonder that the stronger skating nations are exporting pairs skaters to other countries.

Jamie Sale & David Pelletier

The old rule says that you don't get a second chance at a golden opportunity. Luckily for Jamie Sale and David Pelletier, and for pairs skating, there are exceptions to every rule.

In 1996 when Sale was competing in singles and Pelletier was between partners, their respective coaches thought they might make a perfect pairs team. Their physiques matched, they were both good jumpers, and they were both confident, driven athletes.

"But we both still had some growing up to do," Pelletier says of their first, "disastrous" tryout. Sale still shivers at the thought of what could have been, or not been. "What if we didn't get together?"

The skating world would not have seen two of the most evocative pairs programs of all time: 2000's *Love Story* and the mesmerizing interpretation of *Tristan and Isolde* which won the 2001 world championship. Pairs skating might not have taken the quantum leap forward that it did in the new millennium, when not only great tricks but passionate, communicative programs would be required. And Canada would not have had its newest athletic heroes.

With their striking looks, elegant lines, emotional chemistry and flawless musical sense, Sale and Pelletier are such a natural fit that they seemed destined for each other. But destiny sometimes works slowly.

Pelletier grew up in the small eastern Quebec town of Sayabec and from an early age he showed that he was an exceptional athlete. He excelled at swimming and skating, but his mother Murielle made him choose one sport. He selected skating. "I can remember Tuesday nights, my mother hauled me out the door," he laughs. "I had to do figures and dance."

He competed in singles and pairs with astonishing success. He was men's silver medalist at the 1992 Junior Nationals and took bronze the next year. At the same time he won the Canadian novice and junior pairs championship with Julie Laporte. In senior, he teamed with Allison Gaylor and they were the surprise silver medalists at 1995 Nationals, and went on to finish 15th at Worlds. After the

There is a special chemistry between Jamie and David which adds great depth to their presentations.

Born: April 21, 1977, Calgary;
November 22, 1974, Sayabec, Quebec

Hometowns: Red Deer, Alberta;
Sayabec, Quebec

Training Site: Edmonton

Coach: Jan Ullmark

Choreographer: Lori Nichol

RESULTS

1998: 3rd Skate Canada
3rd NHK

1999: 1st Skate America
2nd Sparkassen Cup
2nd Canadian Nationals

2000: 4th Worlds
5th Grand Prix Final
1st Four Continents
1st Skate America
1st Skate Canada
2nd Trophee Lalique
1st Canadian Nationals

2001: 1st Worlds
1st Grand Prix Final
1st Four Continents
1st Canadian Nationals

- When Jamie and David became the sixth Canadian pair to win Worlds, five former Canadian World Champion pairs skaters were in the audience.

- Jamie and David left Montreal in June, 2001 to train in Edmonton with Jan Ullmark.

Worlds | Vancouver | March 2001

FIGURESKATING 77

failed tryout with Sale in 1996—"our egos were both too big at the time" he recalls—he skated with Caroline Roy and they finished a disappointing sixth at Nationals.

"I had become too cocky," Pelletier admits. "And then suddenly you're off the National team and you need to learn from that. I would be stupid if I had to learn that twice."

Sale was going through the same educational process. She started skating in Red Deer, Alberta, when she was five. She also liked gymnastics but her mother, Patti Siegel, made her choose one sport, and Sale went with skating. She concentrated on singles and eventually moved to the famous Royal Glenora Club in Edmonton. Skaters there remember her as a skilled athlete who loved the sport's showmanship.

Coach Cynthia Ullmark suggested she try pairs with Jason Turner and the team had instant success. They won a bronze medal in novice, then took the national junior championship in 1992. In 1994, they were senior bronze medalists and skated at both the Olympics (12th) and Worlds (16th). But at the end of the season the partnership dissolved.

Sale went back to singles and in her first season won bronze at Junior Nationals and finished 12th at Junior Worlds. After not qualifying for Nationals the next year, she nearly quit skating. But she did some soul searching and rediscovered her enthusiasm.

"When you hit rock bottom, that's when you realize you want to skate for the love of the sport," Sale recalls.

And when Pelletier was searching for a new partner again in 1998, this time Sale was ready. She moved to Montreal and the potential of the new team was apparent from the beginning. "I think we both had the same kind of history," Pelletier says.

And they both skated from the heart, something that cannot be taught. Coach Richard Gauthier, whom they left after the 2001 season, worked with Pelletier on being more considerate and appreciative as a pairs partner, and soon the transformation to mature adults was complete.

Sale and Pelletier finished second in their first Nationals together, but had to miss Worlds because of Pelletier's recurring back problems. The next year, though, they burst onto the world scene with *Love Story*, a signature piece choreographed by Lori Nichol. They beat Elena Berezhnaya and Anton Sikharulidze, the reigning world champions, at Skate America, the season's first major event. Later, they won their first Canadian championship, receiving five perfect marks in presentation from the seven judges, some of whom could be seen wiping tears from their eyes.

"In pairs we talk about side-by-side unison and mirror unison," says their choreographer Lori Nichol. "What about spiritual unison? The greatest thing about two people on ice is when they can move as one. And that's what Jamie and David can do."

In 2001, the pair had a superb season, coming from behind to win Skate Canada, and the Grand Prix Final, over Berezhnaya and Sikharulidze. It was also a season of overcoming other issues. They acknowledged that they had become partners off the ice as well as on. Nichol had to top the untoppable *Love Story* and did it with the mature, emotionally demanding *Tristan and Isolde*. When they returned from the Grand Prix Final, they found that a wall of their home had burned, so they had to stay with friends for a few weeks. Then on the day they left for Worlds, Pelletier's car was stolen.

It was time for a good omen, and they found one in Barbara Underhill, the 1984 pairs champion for Canada, who took a wrong turn on her daily jog the morning of the freeskate at Worlds. She came across Sale and Pelletier having breakfast at an outdoor cafe and said to herself, "this moment means something." So she told them of her gold medal skate and how important it was to find peace amid the bedlam of expectations.

That night, Sale and Pelletier found peace. They delivered their program with seamless brilliance and created bedlam in the pro-Canadian arena at Vancouver in the final minute of their world championship skate, just as Underhill and Paul Martini had done 17 years before them.

They had been given a second chance at a golden opportunity and made the most of it.

Elena Berezhnaya & Anton Sikharulidze

It's no wonder Elena Berezhnaya and Anton Sikharulidze are such good jumpers. They've had to clear hurdles all of their lives.

None of the world's top pairs teams has faced as many obstacles as the two-time world champions: a near-fatal accident; a move to a new continent and culture; losing a major championship to cough syrup; and bearing the crushing weight of Russia's fabulous pairs skating history.

Russian teams have won the pairs' gold at each of the last 10 Olympics, and have dominated the world championships since 1965. When Berezhnaya and Sikharulidze joined forces in St. Petersburg in 1996, skating experts assumed Russia had forged the next link in that strong chain.

They were right. By February 1998, Berezhnaya and Sikharulidze were Olympic silver medalists. Five weeks later, they were world champions. And in 1999, they were champions again. But just 25 months before their first world title, not only was the partnership unimaginable, so was the idea that Berezhnaya would ever skate again.

In January 1996, Berezhnaya was at a deserted rink in Riga Latvia, practicing side-by-side camel spins with her former partner Oleg Sliakhov. The spins went horribly wrong and Sliakhov's skate became imbedded in Berezhnaya's head. She underwent emergency brain surgery and spent several weeks recuperating in hospital. There were fears that her speech would be damaged, which it was for a while.

She made a remarkable recovery and a few months later teamed up with Sikharulidze, who had split from his old partner Maria Petrova, with whom he had been ranked sixth in the world.

From the beginning, it was obvious that the new pair had something special. They are blessed with superior speed, they excel at the side-by-side jumps, their

Born: October 1, 1977, Stavropolski; October 25, 1976, Leningrad

Hometown: St. Petersburg, Russia

Training Site: Hackensack, New Jersey

Coach: Tamara Moskvina

Choreographers: Christopher Dean, Igor Bobrin

RESULTS

1998: 2nd Olympics
1st Worlds
1st Europeans
2nd Russian Nationals

1999: 1st Worlds
2nd Grand Prix Final
1st Skate Canada

2000: 3rd Grand Prix Final
1st Cup of Russia
2nd Skate Canada

2001: 2nd Worlds
2nd Grand Prix Final
1st Europeans

- Elena finished seventh in the world in 1994 and 1995, representing Latvia with Oleg Sliakhov; Anton finished sixth in the world in 1995 with Maria Petrova.

Skate Canada | Mississauga | November 2000

Canadian Open | Mississauga | December 1999
Elena and Anton are great storytellers. Above, they peform their famed Charlie Chaplin routine.

FIGURESKATING   81

triple twist is spectacular, and despite their size difference, from the first practice their blade strokes were equal and precise. Their skating has a natural softness and fluidity, which drew immediate comparisons to Ekaterina Gordeeva and the late Sergei Grinkov, the best pairs skaters of the past quarter-century.

Like all new pairs, Berezhnaya and Sikharulidze required time, but not much time, to learn how to compete together. Affected by nerves and unfamiliarity, they finished only ninth in their world championship debut in 1997. However, that autumn, they won the Grand Prix Final, and were suddenly cast into the role of medal contenders for the Nagano Olympics. Just moments from the end of their Olympic freeskate, they crumpled on a lift, and settled for a silver medal. The next month, they put it all together and were runaway winners of the 1998 world championships.

They were in a class by themselves again in 1999, but after that season their coach, the popular Tamara Moskvina, moved from Russia to Hackensack, New Jersey. Berezhnaya and Sikharulidze followed, but it was a difficult adjustment. "They were in a different country, with unfamiliar language and customs," explained Moskvina, herself a former pairs world silver medalist. "Just figuring out how to rent an apartment, get a car, write cheques, where to shop—it was all tough." And Berezhnaya missed her mother Tatiana, who was still in St. Petersburg. The new stresses took their toll. The pair didn't skate as well as they had in their first two seasons together, and often argued over the smallest things.

As they accustomed themselves to their new lives, their performances improved, and they won the European Championships. Three days before the 2000 Worlds, Berezhnaya found out that some cough medicine she had innocently taken to battle bronchitis prior to Europeans contained ephedrine, a banned substance. The pair were stripped of the European title and withdrew from Worlds. It was a devastating experience, but it toughened them and drew them closer together.

Sikharulidze is philosophical. "The whole season started on the wrong foot. It was probably meant to be. Sure it was difficult, but it's life. Others have problems. Now we don't look back, just ahead. I think it's made us stronger, these problems."

Of the two, Sikharulidze speaks the better English; he also creates the ideas for most of their costumes, which are then taken to a designer. Berezhnaya has studied karate and attends art classes to develop her talent at drawing caricatures. They have settled into life in America and it shows in their skating.

They became more flamboyant in their programs for the 2000–01 season, particularly their Charlie Chaplin freeskate. Sikharulidze, particularly, captured the essence of the silent film comedian. All season, they battled for the No. 1 ranking with Canadians Jamie Sale and David Pelletier. After their short program at Worlds, Berezhnaya and Sikharulidze received a standing ovation from the Canadian audience, even though they had beaten Sale and Pelletier. They were cheered wildly again after their Chaplin freeskate, but Sale and Pelletier took the gold with a 6–3 split of judges on the best night of pairs skating most people had ever witnessed.

"We finished second, but we did not lose," Sikharulidze said, and everyone agreed with him.

Many pairs skaters dream about skating like Berezhnaya and her partner. Even their fiercest Olympic rivals admire their ability.

"They have such wonderful lines," says 2001 world champion Jamie Sale. "I just love watching them skate."

Everyone does.

Xue Shen & Hongbo Zhao

Nearly every year, Xue Shen and Hongbo Zhao add another item to their long list of "firsts."

The dynamic pairs team, who have arguably the best throws in the history of the sport, were the first Chinese pair to win a major international event, when they captured NHK in 1997. They were the winners of the first Four Continents Championships, held at Halifax in 1999. That was also the first ISU championship ever won by a Chinese pair. That same season they became the first Chinese pair to win a world medal, with their silver at Worlds in Helsinki. And in 2000, they won the Grand Prix Final, the first Chinese skaters to do that.

The fleet-footed couple have become the trend-setters for a growing legion of Chinese pairs, but when Shen and Zhao were starting, they had no role models to imitate.

Shen and Zhao are both from the northern city of Harbin, often called the coldest city in China. There were two rinks, but only one of them was heated, and the ice was far harder than figure skaters like it because the arenas were also used for speed skating and hockey.

Shen was a somewhat frail child and her parents registered her in skating at the age of eight in the hopes that she would grow stronger. She began her career as a singles skater.

Zhao, whose father is a violinist and mother is a worker in a textile factory, started skating when he was six. He was playing basketball when skating coach Bin Yao noticed how well he moved and suggested he take up skating. Zhao was partnered with Maomao Xie and finished 11th at Junior Worlds, but in 1992 Yao decided to break up the pair and teamed Zhao with Shen. He was 18 and she was only 13.

Born: November 13, 1978, Harbin; September 22, 1973, Harbin

Hometown: Harbin

Training Site: Beijing

Coach: Bin Yao

Choreographers: Sandra Bezic, Michael Siebert, Lea Ann Miller, Gorsha Sur

RESULTS

1997: 11th Worlds
1st NHK
3rd Trophee Lalique
1st Chinese Nationals

1998: 4th Worlds
4th Grand Prix Final
2nd NHK
2nd Cup of Russia
1st Chinese Nationals

1999: 2nd Worlds
1st Four Continents
2nd Cup of Russia
4th NHK
3rd Sparkassen Cup
1st Chinese Nationals

2000: 2nd Worlds
2nd Skate America
2nd Cup of Russia
1st NHK

2001: 3rd Worlds
2nd Four Continents
1st Chinese Nationals

Worlds | Vancouver
March 2001

• After each competition Xue and Hongbo meticulously analyze every part of their programs, to see where they can improve for the next event.

◀ Worlds | Vancouver | March 2001
Xue and Hongbo are athletic and technically accomplished; they deliver astonishing split-second moves.

Worlds | Vancouver | March 2001

Worlds | Vancouver | March 2001

Although Yao had skated pairs internationally (finishing 15th at 1980 Worlds, the first time China competed in pairs), there wasn't much history of the discipline in China. So Zhao and Shen studied videotapes of the world's top teams, dissecting every move. In their second season together they won the National Championship and in 1994, entered their first Worlds, finishing a distant 21st. After a year off because of an injury to Zhao, they returned to finish 15th at 1996 Worlds.

The pair always drew attention because of how far, and how high, Zhao heaved the fearless Shen in their pairs

throws. They were also very competent individual jumpers. But they struggled with other elements such as spins and lifts. And there was very little true unison on the ice.

But Shen and Zhao were eager students and kept working at their shortcomings. They won their first international at NHK in 1997, and a few months later, their magnificent athleticism carried them to fourth place at the 1998 Worlds, seven spots better than the previous year.

They followed that up with their Four Continents win in 1999 and a controversial runner-up finish to reigning world champions Elena Berezhnaya and Anton Sikharulidze at

Worlds | Vancouver | March 2001

the 1999 Worlds in Helsinki. Shen and Zhao received the only standing ovation of the freeskate and many observers, including several of their opponents, thought the Chinese were the best pair in that competition.

"I believe they gave a good enough performance. They could have won it," said Paul Wirtz, then coach of Canadian champions Kristy Sargeant and Kris Wirtz. "It's sad to see such a performance not respected. There wasn't a stumble. We all could have walked under their throws, they were so high. This is pairs skating that we may never see again."

Shen and Zhao had spent time training in Russia and in Simsbury, Connecticut, so they weren't shy about seeking international help. Because their presentation marks were holding them back, in 1999 they came to prominent Toronto choreographer Sandra Bezic, who works with several skaters and is also the creative director for Stars on Ice, the world's leading professional show. Respected American choreographer Michael Siebert also took part in the sessions.

"They were wonderful, but it was very, very difficult because of the language barrier and time constraints,"

said Bezic, who had to speak to the pair through an interpreter. "Everything was new to them, the concept of choreography, the way we worked. They didn't grow up with any of this."

Because they were getting used to certain choreography concepts for the first time, and because they'd missed a month of training when Shen broke her nose in a collision with another skater during practice, the pair had a shaky start to the 1999–2000 season. But they had it together by the Grand Prix Final, which they won, and Worlds, where they finished second.

For the 2000–01 season, Shen and Zhao added a second side-by-side triple jump and at Worlds, on what may have been the finest night of pairs skating ever, they won the bronze medal. But their freeskate would have been good enough to win on almost any other night.

"We have done as asked and improved our artistry," said a disappointed Shen. "We will just have to keep working hard."

Just as they've done throughout their careers.

Marina Petrova & Alexei Tikhonov

When your country has captured all but six of the last 35 world pairs championships, the expectations feel like a block of cement on your shoulders. But in March 2000 Marina Petrova and Alexei Tikhonov withstood the immense pressure to provide Russia with its usual reward: its 30th world pairs title in 36 years.

Petrova and Tikhonov weren't the favorites among the world's top pairs. They weren't even the favorites among their own country's top pairs. That label was worn by two-time world champions Elena Berezhnaya and Anton Sikharulidze, but when she tested positive for banned ingredients in a cough syrup, the pair forfeited their European title to Petrova and Tikhonov, who had won the silver medal. Berezhnaya and Sikharulidze also dropped out of the world championships in Nice, France, leaving Petrova and Tikhonov with the burden of continuing Russian dominance.

"It doesn't matter who is favored," Tikhonov says. "When we compete we're always believing there can be just one place: the first place."

Petrova and Tikhonov made good on their beliefs. While the rest of the field struggled, their acrobatic lifts and throws carried them to the world title, just 21 months after they formed their partnership.

It was a long and winding road, filled with other partners and lots of medals, that led to their union. Ironically, Petrova first attracted international attention skating with Sikharulidze. They won the 1994 and 1995 world junior championships together, but he was determined to skate with Berezhnaya, and left Petrova in 1996. She then paired with Teimuraz Pulin for two years, and they won a silver medal at the 1997 junior Worlds. That partnership didn't have much spark and when Pulin eventually developed health problems, Petrova called Tikhonov.

It had been a long time since Tikhonov had competed for Russia. He had moved to Japan for two years to skate with Yukiko Kawasaki; they had good success in 1994, but

Born: November 29, 1977, Leningrad; November, 1, 1971, Samara
Hometown: St. Petersburg
Training Site: St. Petersburg
Coach: Ludmila Velikova
Choreographer: Sergei Petukhov

RESULTS

1999: 4th Worlds
1st Europeans
1st Sparkassen Cup
1st Cup of Russia

2000: 1st Worlds
1st Europeans
2nd Sparkassen Cup
3rd NHK

2001: 4th Worlds
4th Europeans

- Alexei likes downhill skiing, but he can't do it during the skating season because it's too dangerous. Maria favors reading and playing with her cocker spaniel Bessy.

he returned to Russia later that year to turn professional.

"It was a mistake," he recalls. "I like competition. It's hard, but it's beautiful."

They were fourth in their first Worlds, but in their sophomore season they won three Grand Prix events and capped off the year with their world championship. With their coach Ludmila Velikova, they continue to improvise, especially on their lifts. "We get new ideas," Petrova says. "And we're always working on them."

Skate Canada | Mississauga | November 2000

Complex lifts and dismounts are Marina and Alexei's signature.

Kyoko Ina &
John Zimmerman

She grew up in New York, and competed internationally for Japan. He was raised in Alabama, where ice is what you use to keep your tea cold. Together, they skate for a famous Russian coach. Kyoko Ina and John Zimmerman are definitely not a traditional pairs team.

"We have stories to tell that certainly aren't the same," Ina says. "That keeps our relationship so healthy."

Ina and Zimmerman were already mature adults and experienced international pairs skaters by the time they formed their partnership in 1998. Ina had won two U.S. titles and finished a lofty fourth in the Nagano Olympics with Jason Dungjen. Zimmerman and Stephanie Stiegler had climbed as high as 15th in the World.

When their previous partnerships broke up and Ina and Zimmerman got together, their expectations were probably too high. "It was just a total mismatch at the beginning, neither one of us felt very comfortable," Zimmerman confesses.

But they found a coach with similarly towering goals. Tamara Moskvina, who coaches two-time world champions Elena Berezhnaya and Anton Sikharulidze, had just moved from St. Petersburg, Russia, to Hackensack, New Jersey. Ina and Zimmerman moved there too.

"Tamara organized our thoughts and our direction a little more constructively toward our goals," Ina said.

"Skating with Elena and Anton helped them realize what we were demanding in the way of relating to each other, as partner to partner," Moskvina explains. "John is very spontaneous and Kyoko is very disciplined, so we needed to prepare their timing, their directional movement." She definitely got them moving in the right direction.

Zimmerman says that his partner "is one of the most talented skaters out there right now," and praises her versatility and athleticism. Ina comes by that naturally. Her mother was on the Japanese national swim team, her grandfather ran track at the 1924 Olympics and her grandmother played tennis at Wimbledon.

Zimmerman learned to skate as a three-year-old on a tiny rink at a mall in Birmingham. Growing up, his skating idol was Olympic champion Artur Dmitriev, who trains at the same rink and choreographed Ina's and

Four Continents | Salt Lake City
February 2001

Born: October 11, 1972, Tokyo, Japan; November, 26, 1973, Birmingham, Alabama

Hometown: New York; Birmingham

Training Site: Hackensack, N.J.

Coach: Tamara Moskvina; Igor Moskvin

Choreographers: Tamara Moskvina, Artur Dmitriev, David Audish

RESULTS

1999:
9th Worlds
2nd Skate Canada
4th Trophee Lalique
2nd U.S. Nationals

2000:
7th Worlds
2nd Four Continents
4th Cup of Russia
3rd Trophee Lalique
4th Skate America
1st U.S. Nationals

2001:
7th Worlds
3rd Four Continents
3rd Japan Open
1st U.S. Nationals

• Although she grew up in the U.S.A., Kyoko skated internationally in junior singles for Japan, then returned to win the U.S. junior singles title in 1989 before concentrating on pairs.

Zimmerman's 2001 freeskate. There is Olympic experience everywhere in the arena.

"We're continuing to go to school (in skating) and our degree will hopefully be the Olympics," Zimmerman says.

◀ Four Continents | Salt Lake City | February 2000
Strength, flexibility and creativity define this fascinating pair

Kris and Kristy

Kris Wirtz and Kristy Sargeant-Wirtz consider figure skating their occupation, not their pre-occupation.

That's because they've got other joys and obligations in life. When they come home from a tough practice, they can't dwell on their skating problems because their nine-year-old daughter Triston is waiting for them.

"She's absolutely the most important thing to us," said Kris, who has been captain of the Canadian national team for four years.

The Wirtzes like to describe their skating career together as a roller-coaster ride, and the peaks and valleys were never more obvious than during the 2000–01 season. They changed training rinks from Montreal to Ottawa after leaving their longtime coach Paul Wirtz, Kris's brother, who felt they had reached a plateau under his leadership. Every Monday morning the Wirtzes would leave Montreal, and Triston, to train with Marina Zueva in Ottawa until Thursday.

"Because we sacrificed so much, it actually gave us more motivation in skating," says Kristy.

At both the 2001 Canadian and World championships, the Wirtzes delivered stunning freeskates to the theme from *Far and Away* that left audiences alternately crying and cheering. And both times they needed such brilliant performances after disappointing short programs. At Worlds, they finished a strong eighth overall, their fifth time among the world's top 10.

Kristy Sargeant and Kris Wirtz teamed up in 1993. They were Canadian runners-up three times before winning their first of two national titles in 1998. Often, their appearances at Nationals were marked by bizarre occurences. In 1995, Kris could hardly breathe because of pneumonia. In 1996, he spent the night before the freeskate in hospital after suffering a serious concussion from a fall during practice. Then the arena fire alarm went off during their freeskate. In 1997, Kristy's elbow almost knocked Kris out during the long program.

Kris and Kristy have always had excellent spins and exemplary speed and many skating experts say their death spiral is the best in the world. What's kept them from the world podium is, according to Kris, "I'm not the biggest male pairs skater. Far from it."

Born: January 24, 1974, Red Deer, Alberta (Kristy); December 12, 1969 Thunder Bay, Ontario (Kris)

Hometown: Delson, Quebec

Training Site: Ottawa

Coach: Marina Zueva

Choreographer: Marina Zueva

RESULTS

1997: 6th Worlds
5th Skate Canada
4th Trophee Lalique
2nd Canadian Nationals

1998: 12th Olympics
7th Worlds
5th Goodwill Games
2nd Skate America
4th Skate Canada
4th Trophee Lalique
1st Canadian Nationals

1999: 6th Worlds
2nd Four Continents
3rd Skate Canada
5th Trophee Lalique
1st Canadian Nationals

2000: 10th Worlds
4th Four Continents
2nd Canadian Nationals

2001: 8th Worlds
7th Four Continents
2nd Canadian Nationals

Worlds | Vancouver | March 2001

• Kris and Kristy became engaged in 1997 on Canada Day (July 1) and were married two years later.

Before the 2001 season Kristy wanted to return to a more "normal" life but kept competing, "because she's doing this for me," Kris says. "She's been there for me. I'll be there for her."

They've always been there for each other.

Kris and Kristy often add highly lyrical accents to their skating.

Tatiana Totmianina & Maxim Marinin

It can never be said that Tatiana Totmianina and Maxim Marinin fear change. It seems they thrive on it.

They switched coaches just three weeks before the 2001 World Championships. They moved from Russia to the U.S. Earlier, they converted from singles skaters to pairs skaters. So they probably can handle the necessary transformation from athletes to performers.

"Yes, of course, we need to work hard on our artistry," says Marinin. "With our new coach, we'll find that direction. I think our strength in pairs is our jumps."

Everyone else thinks that too. Unlike most pairs, they each have mastery of two triples, the toe loop and the Salchow. And they've also tried side-by-side triple Lutzes in competition, although they didn't land them.

It's not surprising that this pair can jump. Totmianina was a singles skater in her native St. Petersburg, Russia, until 1996 when she and Marinin formed their partnership. Marinin had moved into pairs after he was beaten by Evgeny Plushenko, five years younger, in a competition in Volgograd.

Totmianina and Marinin trained in St. Petersburg on the same ice as world champions Maria Petrova and Alexei Tikhonov, "which was very useful, because we could watch each other," says Marinin. But despite that comfort level and a major breakthrough to a silver medal at the 2001 Europeans, the pair had differences with coach Natalia Pavlova. Just before Worlds, they left St. Petersburg for Chicago, to work with Oleg Vasiliev, who won the 1984 Olympic gold with partner Elena Valova. But Vasiliev couldn't come to Vancouver for Worlds, so they consulted with him by phone.

Totmianina and Marinin say they'll continue to train in Chicago, and will remain eligible after the 2002

Born: November, 2, 1981, Perm; March 23, 1977, Volgograd

Hometown: St. Petersburg

Training Site: Chicago

Coach: Oleg Vasiliev

Choreographer: Natalia Pavlova

RESULTS

1998: 5th Trophee Lalique
2nd Skate Israel
5th Russian Nationals

1999: 7th Worlds
5th Europeans
2nd Trophee Lalique
3rd Cup of Russia
3rd Russian Nationals

2000: 6th Worlds
5th Europeans
3rd Russian Nationals
3rd Sparkassen Cup
3rd Skate America

2001: 5th Worlds
2nd Europeans
3rd Russian Nationals

Worlds | Vancouver | March 2001
This pair is physically perfectly matched; they move as one.

• Maxim is a student at the Physical Academy of Sport in St. Petersburg and will try to continue his studies, even though the pair has moved to Chicago. Tatiana is graduating from the School of Olympic in St. Petersburg, a special school for athletes which offers modified schedules.

Games. By then, they should have side-by-side triple Lutzes, which would force other pairs to be the ones making changes.

Dorota Zagorska & Mariusz Siudek

To understand just how committed Dorota Zagorska and Mariusz Siucek are to their pairs partnership, it is necessary to know something about May 13, 2000. It's their wedding day.

"It was our only day off from training," Zagorska explains. "We were back on the ice the next day."

Zagorska and Siudek don't like to skip practice, even for a wedding, because ice time has been at a premium during their careers. They used to spend three weeks of every summer at a rink in Chicago because no arena in Poland had summer ice.

"But now, we train only in Oswiecim, our rink is good there," Siudek says proudly. "Our hockey team just won the Polish championship (in 2001)."

So Zagorska and Siudek finally have some local company in their celebrity status. The couple are the only Polish pairs team to win a medal at the world championship, a bronze at Helsinki in 1999. Their performance at 2001 Worlds would have been medal-caliber in almost any other year, but the freeskate at Vancouver was the deepest pairs skating competition in world-championship history. The crowd gave the Polish pair a rousing standing ovation, but they finished sixth.

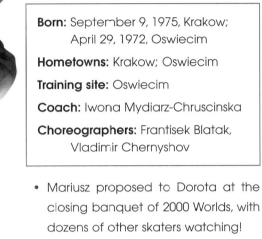

Worlds | Vancouver | March 2001

"But it was the first time we skated both short and long clean this season, so we're happy," Siudek said.

They want their international success to inspire younger Polish skaters. They

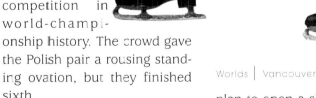

Worlds | Vancouver
March 2001

Strong lifts characterize this exciting pair.

Born: September 9, 1975, Krakow;
    April 29, 1972, Oswiecim

Hometowns: Krakow; Oswiecim

Training site: Oswiecim

Coach: Iwona Mydiarz-Chruscinska

Choreographers: Frantisek Blatak,
    Vladimir Chernyshov

• Mariusz proposed to Dorota at the closing banquet of 2000 Worlds, with dozens of other skaters watching!

RESULTS

1998: 10th Olympics
5th Worlds
4th Europeans
3rd Goodwill Games

1999: 3rd Worlds
2nd Europeans
3rd NHK
3rd Trophee Lalique

2000: 5th Worlds
3rd Europeans
3rd Cup of Russia
4th Skate Canada

2001: 6th Worlds
4th Grand Prix Final

plan to open a skating school in Oswiecim, based on the Russian model.

"There are only eight ice rinks working for 10 months a year in Poland," Siudek says. "There are more than that in Vancouver alone.

"When we started, there was just a wish that we wanted to try skating. There were no such things as role models."

There are now.

Tiffany Scott & Philip Dulebohn

After test-driving their partnership for a week, Tiffany Scott thought she'd try skating with John Dulebohn, "just for the summer."

They must have long summers in Delaware. Five years later, Scott and Dulebohn were still together and had finished ninth in the 2000 Worlds.

"I just wanted to let it soak in and relish it," Dulebohn recalls. "Because you never know when you're going to be in the top 10 in the world."

In the beginning, even qualifying for the Worlds seemed to be out of the question. At their first junior regional competition, Scott and Dulebohn placed last among the five entrants, the kind of discouraging result which can lead to a quick breakup.

"We had a rough start," Scott concedes. "It took us a while to click."

But they had faith in each other and stuck it out. They got along well together, and they are strong individual skaters because each had experience in singles. Their confidence in the partnership was rewarded with a bronze medal at the 1997 Junior Nationals.

"That was a big moment," Dulebohn agrees. "We proved ourselves that day."

They kept proving themselves, eventually jumping onto the podium with a silver medal in 2000, immediately followed by a bronze at Four Continents. That foreshadowed their breakthrough into the top 10 at Worlds.

"I don't think people anticipated us getting to this point when we started," Dulebohn said.

Seven years after that initial tryout, they were favorites to make the Olympic team. That's well beyond "just for the summer."

▲ Four Continents | Salt Lake City | February 2001
Tiffany's carriage makes Philip's high lifts beautiful.

Born: May 1, 1977, Weymouth, Massachusetts; September 13, 1973, Silver Springs, Maryland

Hometowns: Hanson, Massachusetts; Germantown, Maryland

Training Site: Newark, Delaware

Coach: Karl Kurtz

Choreographer: Ron Luddington

RESULTS

1999: 6th Four Continents
6th Skate America
6th Trophee Lalique
5th U.S. Nationals

2000: 9th Worlds
3rd Four Continents
8th Cup of Russia
2nd U.S. Nationals

2001: 11th Worlds
3rd Four Continents
2nd U.S. Nationals

• Tiffany started skating at age four, while John was five when he took to the ice.

Four Continents | Salt Lake City
February 2001

Worlds | Vancouver
March 2001

Sarah Abitbol &
Stephane Bernadis

The tradition of pairs skating in France is like the tradition of sun-tanning at the North Pole.

There isn't one.

When Sarah Abitbol and Stephane Bernadis powered their way to a bronze medal at the 2000 Worlds, it was the first world pairs medal for France in 68 years. What made the 2000 medal more remarkable was that the day before, Bernadis had his left forearm slashed by an unknown assailant in the doorway of his hotel room. He received four stitches in the arm and was surrounded by heavy security—an emotionally draining experience. The excitement seemed to suit a couple known for its dramatic approach to the sport. They have often been compared to ice dancers for their artistry and expression.

Abitbol took to the ice at six; she liked pairs but also skated singles, finishing 21st at Junior Worlds in 1993. Bernadis's mother, Donna Davies, was a former member of the British National skating team, and she encouraged her eight-year-old son to take up the sport. He decided upon pairs because he didn't think he'd succeed in singles. Abitbol and Bernadis got together at a tryout camp in 1992 and by 1994 they had won their first of eight consecutive French championships. Their specialty is throw jumps, and they have been working on the unprecedented throw triple Axel.

"I want to jump," says the fiery Abitbol. "I don't want to just keep my skates on the ice."

In 1999 the pair began training in Paris under Stanislav Leonovich, who also coached the legendary Gordeeva and Grinkov. "Being coached by a Russian gives us credit," Bernadis said.

Their hope is to eventually open a pairs training center and develop a French pairs tradition that did not exist until they arrived.

◆ Worlds | Vancouver | March 2001
This team has technical ability and a great sense of humor.

Born: June 8, 1975, Nantes; February 23, 1974, Boulogne Billancourt

Hometowns: Paris; Bougival

Training Site: Paris

Coach: Stanislav Leonovich

Choreographer: Stanislav Leonovich

RESULTS

1998: 6th Olympics
8th Worlds
3rd Europeans
4th Grand Prix Final
6th Goodwill Games
1st Trophee Lalique
1st French Nationals

1999: 5th Worlds
3rd Europeans
1st Trophee Lalique
2nd NHK
1st French Nationals

2000: 3rd Worlds
3rd Europeans
2nd Grand Prix Final
1st Sparkassen Cup
2nd NHK
4th Trophee Lalique
1st French Nationals

2001: (Withdrew, injury) Worlds
3rd Europeans
5th Grand Prix Final
1st French Nationals

• In the summer of 1992 Bernardis teamed with Surya Bonaly, but she decided to concentrate on singles (very successfully).

• Abitbol began skating at school at six, when she had to choose between that sport and swimming for physical education.

THE DANCE TEAMS

Barbara Fusar Poli and Maurizio Margaglio

Marina Anissina and Gwendal Peizerat

Shae-Lynn Bourne and Victor Kraatz

Irina Lobacheva and Ilia Averbukh

Margarita Drobiazko and Povilas Vanagas

Galit Chait and Sergei Sakhnovski

Kati Winkler and Rene Lohse

Elena Grushina and Ruslan Goncharov

Naomi Lang and Peter Tchernyshev

Marie-France Dubreuil and Patrice Lauzon

Isabelle Delobel and Olivier Schoenfelder

Albena Denkova and Maxim Staviyski

Tanith Belbin and Benjamin Agosto

Since it became an Olympic event in 1976, ice dancing has been plagued by severe judging controversies, rigid rankings and monopolization by one country.

But it is almost always the first skating event sold out at the Olympic Games.

To many fans, dancing is the most entertaining discipline in skating. It is certainly the most theatrical. Because

ice dancers are freed from the burden of landing difficult individual jumps or dangerous pairs throws, there is more room for creativity and expression. The accent is on rhythm, translating precise dance-floor steps to the faster medium of ice, and showcasing two people united in their interpretation of music.

Ice dancing differs from pairs and singles skating in a number of ways. The costumes are more elaborate, and the story-telling in the programs more complex. With only a few brief exceptions, the partners must maintain contact with each other throughout the dance, and one foot of each skater must be on the ice. There are no jumps, which separates the way dancers practice from the way other skaters train. As a result, ice dancers tend to be of different body shapes—taller and leaner, generally—and athletic temperaments than singles skaters.

And ice dance is the only discipline which has retained a "compulsory" segment. Singles skating got rid of compulsory figures in 1990, and pairs never had them. But at the start of every season, ice dancers are given a list of four compulsory dances, and at major competitions, two must be performed, each worth 10 per cent of the final mark. The Original Dance is worth 30 per cent and must be skated to a certain rhythm (tango, polka, blues, etc.), but the skaters design their own programs. The freedance, worth 50 per cent, can be skated to any music and allows the couples to unleash the full forces of their speed and creativity.

After complaints about judging peaked at the 1998 Winter Olympics, the rules of ice dancing became more formalized. Judging panels are chosen only at the last minute. Falls and stumbles are now penalized, there are limits on the number of separations (five) and small lifts (seven) in a freedance, and certain standard elements are required.

Since ice dancing became part of the World Championships in 1952, it has been dominated by Europeans, first by the British, then the Russians. No North American or Asian couple has ever won Worlds. From 1969 to 1999, couples from Russia or the old Soviet Union won 25 of 31 world titles and six of seven Olympic gold medals.

But that is changing quickly and dramatically.

Marina Anissina and Gwendal Peizerat of France won in 2000 and Barbara Fusar Poli and Maurizio Margaglio gave Italy its first ice dancing world championship in 2001. Canadians Shae-Lynn Bourne and Victor Kraatz have been gold-medal caliber since 1998. Lithuania's Margarita Drobiazko and Povilas Vanagas have a huge following. And even Israel has a medal-contender in Galit Chait and Sergei Sakhnovski. At 2000 Worlds, Russia did not win an ice dance medal for the first time in 36 years.

But Anissina, Sakhnovski and a number of other top finishers were trained in Russia. They represent another ice dancing trend: globalization. When the

Soviet Union dissolved in the early 1990s, it created several new countries such as Lithuania and Ukraine with already strong ice dance traditions. And the legion of well-trained Soviet dancers and coaches were free—and financially compelled—to leave for other countries. Three of the best coaches, Natalia Linichuk, Natalia Dubova and Tatiana Tarasova, emigrated to America. Many of the top Russian couples followed them and other teams flocked to their new training centers.

Of the top 10 ice dance teams at 2001 Worlds, only two (Fusar-Poli/Margaglio and Germany's Kati Winkler and Rene Lohse) were both born in the country they represent, and also train there full time.

The result has been a sharing of ideas, which has created some kind of parity. When the Italians dethroned the French in 2001, it was just the second time in 20 years that a reigning champion had competed for the world title and lost. While champions may change more regularly there is still little movement once a competition starts. The final standing of the first 18 couples after the freedance at 2001 Worlds was exactly the same as it had been after the Original Dance. That goes against common sense and the current depth of talent worldwide.

"I look back to the Olympic year in Nagano [1998] and there were four different teams who were strong," Victor Kraatz said. "Now there are six very good teams. No longer is just one team going to win all the time. Any of six could win any competition."

Barbara Fusar-Poli & Maurizio Margaglio

Maybe the best way to appreciate Barbara Fusar-Poli and Maurizio Margaglio is not to watch them, but to drink them.

"I'm like a bottle of champagne," says the bubbly Fusar-Poli, "Maurizio is quiet, but he is like a bottle of Coke. You shake him up and he is like a bomb."

The Italians certainly exploded onto the world ice dance scene. Only a year after forming their partnership, they finished 10th at the 1996 World Championships, a remarkable debut. By 2001 they were world champions.

In his descriptive English, Margaglio said, "It was an incredible warm coming up from all my body and going into joy," after their passionate Romeo and Juliet freedance edged the Beethoven program by reigning champions Marina Anissina and Gwendeal Peizerat. "I was like a sun shining rays everywhere."

Those rays could be the dawn of a figure skating revival in Italy. Fusar-Poli and Margaglio's gold was the first world championship won by Italy in any figure skating discipline. Prior to the couple's silver medal in the 2000 event, Italy's total skating medal haul at Worlds was two bronzes, the most recent in 1978.

Italians are passionate sports fans, as long as the sport is skiing or soccer. Figure skating has not been featured on live television in Italy for many years. Fusar-Poli and Margaglio hope their victory will influence Italian skating just as Alberto Tomba's Olympic gold medals triggered a skiing boom in Italy. "We won everything, and people are starting to know us," Margaglio says. "Boys and girls are watching our performances. I hope we will be heros for

Born: February 6, 1972, Sesto San Giovanni; November 16, 1974, Milan

Hometown: Sesto San Giovanni; Courmayeur

Training Site: Milano

Coaches: Roberto Pelizzola; Paola Mezzadri, Tatiana Tarasova.

Choreographer: Ludmilla Vlasova

RESULTS

1998: 6th Olympics
5th Worlds
5th Grand Prix Final
5th Europeans
2nd Trophee Lalique
3rd Skate America

1999: 5th Worlds
5th Grand Prix Final
4th Europeans
1st Italian Nationals
1st Cup of Russia
1st Skate America
2nd Trophee Lalique

2000: 2nd Worlds
2nd Grand Prix Final
2nd Europeans
1st Skate America
1st Cup of Russia
1st Japan Open

2001: 1st Worlds
1st Grand Prix Final
1st Europeans

- Barbara finished 17th at the 1994 Worlds with former partner Alberto Reani.

Worlds | Nice | March 2000

The non-stop action and speed of this team leaves you breathless.

them and they will start skating. Our goal is to have Italian TV show the finals, live."

"My parents had to watch us win on French TV!" Fusar-Poli adds.

Soccer was Margaglio's first love. Like most Italian boys, he began playing almost as soon as he could walk. He didn't discover figure skating until he was 10, and then only because it was at an outdoor rink that somehow maintained ice despite the warm weather.

"I had no idea it was a frozen sport," he laughs. "But skating gave me the opportunity to communicate with people. Flying on the ice, feeling the air on my face—it was not like that in soccer. So Italian soccer maybe lost somebody, but maybe skating gained somebody."

Skating gained Fusar-Poli from swimming, after a friend asked her to attend one of his exhibitions. Inspired, she was on the ice the very next day. Ironically, she told her mother—former national champion sprinter Nives Satori—that she wanted to leave swimming because the pool was too cold.

"Stupid!" she says, slapping her forehead in jest. "Now, it's worse! You can't keep warm because our rink in Milan is very cold. Very nice...but very cold."

Their skating, though, is hot. And so was the couple's rise through the usually rigid dancing ranks. After their sizzling 10th place debut at Worlds in 1995, they weren't climbing the world ladder as quickly as they wanted. So before the 1998 season, they sought the help of legendary coach Tatiana Tarasova. They still train nearly 11 months a year in Milan with coaches Roberto Pelizzola and Paola Mezzadri, but they spend an intense month in the U.S. with Tarasova at the start of the season, working on the hundreds of little moves and edge strokes which make up an ice dance program.

"Tatiana does the bricks," says Maurizio. "Then with Paola and Roberto we decide where to put the bricks and how to do the house, and then Ludmilla [Vlasova, the choreographer] is like the painter at the end when the house is built."

Besides the bricks, Tarasova gave them long-term hope. Although they were then ranked ninth, Tarasova said that they would thank her when they eventually won an Olympic title. The pair couldn't believe the prediction, but Tarasova's finishing touches began to pay off with higher placings. Their speed increased noticeably and it became apparent this was no longer an uneven union of the talented, effervescent Fusar-Poli and her quiet partner in the background. Margaglio's skating improved dramatically, and the on-ice interplay between the couple became spicier and more emotional.

At the 2000 Worlds in Nice, their cha-cha won the Original Dance right in front of Anissina and Peizerat's home crowd.

The French couple later swept the freedance to win gold, but the Italians had made a significant statement.

Fusar-Poli and Margaglio work fiendishly during the off-season, spending 10 hours daily together on the ice, dance floor and in dryland training. Italy produces some of the best ballroom dancers in the world, and the couple studies with several of them. All of the labor paid off as the couple went undefeated through the 2000–01 season.

Despite all the time together, they are not a couple off the ice. On June 24, 2000, Fusar-Poli married Diego Cattani, an Olympic short-track speed skater and manager of their Milan ice rink.

Although he has a girlfriend, "on the ice, Barbara is the best woman for me," Margaglio says. "I am trying to play the man role and she is playing the woman role. Easy to say but hard to demonstrate. She gets the best out of you."

Champagne usually does.

Marina Anissina & Gwendal Peizerat

It was probably the most dramatic moment in French figure skating history.

During the final minute of Marina Anissina and Gwendal Peizerat's powerful "Carmina Burana" freedance at the 2000 Worlds, the French couple entered one of their trademark moves, where she lifts and carries him. At the sight of this familiar role reversal, 8000 fans at the arena in Nice, France, rose to their feet in a screaming, hysterical mass. Even though there were still four couples to skate, they were convinced the local heroes had won the world championship. And they were right. The scoreboard was strewn with four 6.0s for presentation and the ice was strewn with more flowers than greeted Napoleon on his return from exile.

"There was so much noise." Peizerat marveled, "that it felt like being in another world."

It was just the second French gold medal won at a world championship held in France. In 1952, when the legendary Jacqueline du Bief skated to the championship in Paris, figure skating was not nearly as popular, nor its stars so universally well known, as today.

For Anissina and Peizerat it was a triumphant performance in the right place at precisely the right time. But the six-time French champions had been building steadily toward this peak since 1993.

They used to compete against each other at Junior Worlds, with different partners and for different countries. Anissina and Ilia Averbukh represented the Soviet Union and won the 1990 and 1993 Junior World title. Peizerat and Marina Morel took a bronze for France at the 1988 Junior Worlds and silver in 1992.

Averbukh left Anissina in 1992 because he had fallen in love with Irina Lobacheva and wanted to skate with her. Unable to find a partner in Russia, Anissina sent letters to some skaters in other countries, including one to Peizerat,

Worlds | Nice | March 2000

Born: August 8, 1975, Moscow; April 21, 1972, Bron

Hometowns: Moscow; Lyon

Training Site: Lyon

Coach: Muriel Boucher-Zazoui

Choreographers: Jayne Torvill, Christopher Dean, Ludmila Vlasova

RESULTS

1997: 5th Worlds
4th Europeans
3rd Grand Prix Final
1st French Nationals

1998: 3rd Olympics
2nd Worlds
3rd Grand Prix Final
3rd Europeans
1st NHK
1st Trophee Lalique
1st Skate America
1st French Nationals

1999: 2nd Worlds
2nd Europeans
2nd Grand Prix Final
1st NHK
1st Trophee Lalique
1st French Nationals

2000: 1st Worlds
1st Europeans
1st Grand Prix Final
1st Skate Canada
1st Trophee Lalique
1st NHK

2001: 2nd Europeans
2nd Worlds

• Marina and Gwenda have often changed their Original Dance mid-season, to improve its character.

⏴ Winter Olympics | Nagano | February 1998
Marina and Gwendal highlight their emotional programs with innovative and challenging moves.

written in French, a language she didn't speak at the time. He didn't respond at first, but when Morel retired from the sport a month later, Peizerat called Anissina.

They decided to skate for France because training facilities were better and the competition not quite so stiff. Anissina moved to Lyon, and boarded with Peizerat's family for the first year until she moved into her own apartment.

The new couple had great differences, not only in language and culture, but in their approach to their sport. Anissina was from the classical Russian school of ice dance; Peizerat's style was more modernist. She has an explosive temperament, while he is cooler and calmer.

"It is a strange chemistry," Peizerat concedes.

But coach Muriel Boucher-Zazoui was able to meld the two opposites into dramatic, electric unison. Each has great foot speed, superior body strength, strong technical skills and an impeccable athletic background.

Peizerat's parents, Monique and Eugene, were ice dancers and Peizerat entered that discipline right away rather than starting in singles. His father is one of the top officials in the French skating federation, his mother runs the local skating club and his sister Sandrine is a skating judge.

Anissina's father, Viacheslav Anissin, won Olympic and world championships with the Soviet Union's hockey team and was a key player in the famous 1972 Summit Series against Canada. Her mother, Irina Chernaeva, skated pairs for the Soviet Union, finishing sixth at the 1972 Olympics, and is now a coach.

When Anissina left for France at the age of 17, her parents didn't think she'd be away for long. But despite some early communication problems, the new partnership flourished. In their first full season together, Anissina and Peizerat finished second at French Nationals, 12th at Europeans and 10th at Worlds. But they could not go to the 1994 Olympics in Lillehammer because Anissina was not yet a French citizen.

As their partnership progressed Anissina learned to speak French fluently and became a French citizen. In between training sessions, both of them attended university. She holds a degree in history and he has a Master's in sports management.

By 1995, the couple had propelled themselves into the world's top six with their distinct speed, contorted, acrobatic lifts and theatrical presentation.

They received their first perfect 6.0 at the 1997 French Nationals, and the next year, even though they had not yet won a world medal, they slipped past Canadians Shae-Lynn Bourne and Victor Kraatz onto the podium at the 1998 Olympics. Their bronze was just the second Olympic medal ever won by French ice dancers. Isabelle and Paul Duchesnay took silver in 1992.

Five weeks after the Olympics, Anissina and Peizerat moved up to the silver medal at Worlds. In 1999, they won silver again but were much closer to gold, losing a controversial split decision to defending world champions Anjelika Krylova and Oleg Ovsiannikov. But there would be no doubt the following year.

In 1999–2000, Anissina and Peizerat enjoyed one of the most successful seasons by any dance team in history. They captured every one of the six major events they entered and lost just one segment, the Original Dance at Worlds. But they recovered with a flamboyant freedance to win the gold medal in their home country. Their majestic freedance was choreographed by famed ice dancer Christopher Dean.

Anissina hurt her back at Europeans in 2001, so the couple dropped out of the Grand Prix Final. When they finished second again to Italians Barbara Fusar-Poli and Maurizio Margaglio at Worlds, Anissina and Peizerat felt they'd skated well enough to win. So did many others.

"We still have to believe in ourselves," said Peizerat. "We must not lose our faith."

With their background of success, there's not much chance of that.

Shae-Lynn Bourne & Victor Kraatz

In the end, whether or not they ever win a world championship, Shae-Lynn Bourne and Victor Kraatz will have had a bigger impact on ice dancing than any couple of their era. They have stayed near the top of their event for longer than other teams of their time; they revitalized North American interest in ice dancing; they injected athleticism and speed into a discipline which had, for many critics, become cheap theater; and they have bequeathed a new element to the sport.

It took years for anyone else to attempt "hydro-blading," the low-to-the-ice, gravity-defying style that Bourne and Kraatz introduced to the world during a practice at the 1994 Winter Olympics. All of the other couples had left the ice, and the audience was leaving too, when Bourne and Kraatz began their hydro-blading drill, moving around the ice at impossible angles, crouched like cats on the prowl. Within seconds, the departing fans, intrigued, returned to their seats. The Canadians incorporated the technique into their competitive programs and it never fails to rouse the audience. It also became the foundation, and inspiration, for many revolutionary athletic moves by other elite dancers, including the concept of the woman carrying the man, a move which Anissina and Peizerat delight in.

Bourne and Kraatz also influenced changes in the way ice dancing is judged. After they skated well but were denied a medal at the 1998 Olympics, new, more definitive rules for marking were introduced by the International Skating Union. Their Riverdance freeskate of that season is still the most memorable ice dance program since France's Duchesnays retired in 1992.

- Shae-Lynn skated courageously through the 1999–2000 season despite severe knee damage which required surgery at the end of the year.

- Victor speaks four languages: English, Italian, German and French.

- In 2001 Shae-Lynn and Victor won their eighth Canadian title tying the record set by Tracy Wilson and Rob McCall.

Born: January 24, 1976, Chatham, Ontario; April 7, 1971, Berlin

Hometowns: Chatham; Vancouver

Training Site: Newington, Connecticut

Coach: Tatiana Tarasova

Choreographers: Tatiana Tarasova, Nikolai Morozov

RESULTS

1997: 3rd Worlds
1st Grand Prix Final
1st Skate Canada
2nd NHK
1st Canadians Nationals

1998: 4th Olympics
3rd Worlds
2nd Grand Prix Final
1st Skate Canada
2nd Sparkassen Cup
1st Canadian Nationals

1999: 3rd Worlds
1st Four Continents
1st Sparkassen Cup
2nd Cup of Russia
1st Canadian Nationals

2000: 5th Grand Prix Final
3rd Sparkassen Cup
3rd Skate America

2001: 4th Worlds
1st Four Continents
1st Canadian Nationals

Worlds | Vancouver | March 2001
Sometimes playful, sometimes poetic, Shae-Lynn and Vic are always masters of superb edge work.

Skate America | Colorado Springs | October 2000

It was in 1992 that Bourne and Kraatz captured their first important title, the Canadian Junior Nationals, despite Bourne's skull fracture. She had to wear a helmet during practices for Canadians. The next year, they won the senior championship, a crown they have relinquished just once, when they had to skip Canadians in 2000 because their season had already ended with Bourne's knee surgery.

Although Bourne and Kraatz enjoyed instant competitive success, their partnership almost didn't happen. In April 1991, Kraatz conducted a cross-country search for a new partner and test-skated with more than a dozen young women without success. After another failed session in Montreal, he was just about to leave the rink when the arena manager suggested he take a spin with a dynamic 16-year-old who was new to ice dancing.

"Five minutes later, Shae-Lynn and I decided to try it for one week, and then I asked her to skate with me," Kraatz recalls. "It's still the best decision I ever made."

It was a great match. They had similar lines, both are very athletic and fast on their feet and they each have what skaters refer to as "soft knees," which allow for smooth, deep strokes. And each had the burning will to achieve.

Bourne was raised in a sports-minded family in the western Ontario town of Chatham, and was originally a pairs skater but loved the rhythm and speed of ice dancing. Her pairs training developed her powerful, athletic form. Kraatz was born in West Berlin, but raised in an Italian-speaking region in Switzerland. His first love was skiing, but he kept injuring himself, so when he was 10 his mother suggested he take skating lessons. He eventually won the Swiss junior ice dance championships before his family moved to Canada in 1987.

Once Bourne and Kraatz found each other, their rise was spectacular. They finished 14th in their world debut in 1993, 10th in the 1994 Olympics and sixth at Worlds a few weeks later. In 1996, they came in third at Worlds in Edmonton, the first podium placing by a North American dance team since Tracy Wilson and Rob McCall in 1988. They also won bronze each of the next three years, the Grand Prix Final in 1997, and 25 international medals, spectacular achievements in a discipline absolutely dominated since its inception by Europeans, on the ice and in the judging panel.

Along the way, Bourne and Kraatz have changed coaches and training sites several times. After the disappointment of the 1998 Olympics and declining results in 1999–2000, culminating in Bourne's season-ending injury, Kraatz considered retiring from the sport. The couple decided to renew their commitment to skating, but also

Champion Series Final | Hamilton | December 1997

decided they needed some kind of fresh start. So they switched from Natalia Dubova, whom they highly respected, to new coach Tatiana Tarasova, in Newington, Connecticut. They trained with leading teams from Israel, Japan and, periodically, the world champions from Italy.

"We have discovered new aspects in skating," Bourne says. "That's not taking anything away from our previous coaches. All our coaches have taken us closer to the end.

"Our biggest desire is to keep on growing."

Bourne and Kraatz returned to competition for the 2000–01 season, after her second knee surgery in two years, trying to re-establish their standing. They were a better-trained couple with more of the emotion and theatrical flair that has characterized European dancers. But they had not abandoned their distinct, quick footwork, hydro-blading and enthusiastic athleticism. Despite missing the previous Worlds, they finished fourth in 2001, missing the podium by one judge. But it's not results which Bourne and Kraatz want as their legacy to the sport.

"We want to be remembered as people who made a change in the ice-dancing world," Kraatz once said. "Who brought the athletic into it and made it more exciting."

Mission accomplished.

Worlds | Vancouver | March 2001

Irina Lobacheva
& Ilia Averbukh

I n every sport with a podium, the most detested finish is fourth place. It's like pressing your nose against the window of the candy store.

Irina Lobacheva and her husband Ilia Averbukh knew that feeling too well. They finished fourth in three straight world championships from 1998–2000, and also in two European championships. And when they fell just short of the podium in 2000, it marked the first time that Russia had not won at least one ice dancing medal at Worlds since 1965.

But Lobacheva and Averbukh began a new Russian streak in 2001, finishing third in the world with their swirling interpretation of Bach's music. It capped a satisfying season in which they also won bronze at Europeans, took silvers at two Grand Prix events and at the Grand Prix Final, and won their second successive national championship.

"Last season, we had too many losses," Averbukh said after their emotional freeskate. "But we became much stronger. We were very nervous at the Worlds, because we skated well all season, but if you don't win a medal, then the whole season doesn't feel right."

So, finally, it felt right. Skating partners since 1992 and married since 1994, Averbukh and Lobacheva finished 13th at their first Worlds in 1994.

"In Russia we were having trouble getting training time and getting enough to eat," Lobacheva recalled. The difficulties were reflected in their world results, as they dropped to 15th in 1995. So they emigrated to Delaware, and the next year, they leapt to sixth at Worlds, a stunning advance in the rigid world of ice dancing.

The couple are reconsidering their original plan to tour professionally after the Salt Lake City Games.

"I think maybe we'll skate for two more years after the Olympics," Averbukh said as he ran his fingers over his first world medal.

Born: February 18, 1973, Ivanteeka; December 18, 1973, Moscow

Hometown: Moscow

Training Site: Newark, Delaware

Coaches: Natalia Linichuk, Gennadi Karponosov

Choreographer: Natalia Linichuk

RESULTS

1998: 5th Olympics
4th Worlds
4th Europeans

1999: 4th Worlds
3rd Europeans

2000: 4th Worlds
4th Europeans

2001: 3rd Worlds
3rd Europeans

• Both Irina and Ilia began as singles skaters. Ilia preferred soccer and hockey, but stayed in skating, and switched to ice dancing when he was 12.

◀ Winter Olympics | Nagano | February 1998

Worlds | Vancouver | March 2001

◀ Winter Olympics | Nagano | February 1998
Irina and Ilia come up with some fabulously improbable dance moves.

Margarita Drobiazko & Povilas Vanagas

Povilas Vanagas says that his first partner was a chair. He was very young and still learning about ice dancing and the chair helped support him. He's still got support from his partner, only now that partner is a human being, and also his wife, Margarita Drobiazko.

After eight years as skating partners, the longtime Lithuanian national champions were married on June 4, 2000, in Moscow.

"Nothing's changed," Drobiazko says. "Our relationship evolved gradually anyway. It's not like we met for the first time at the wedding."

Drobiazko started skating at the age of six, and began training under the legendary Natalia Linichuk when she was 11. She was partnered with Oleg Granionov, then changed to another renowned coach, Natalia Dubova.

When she first teamed with Vanagas, he had had little exposure to ice dancing. He'd been Lithuanian champion in men's singles six times, not quite matching the streak of his mother, Lilia Vanagiene, who won the Lithuanian women's title every year of the 1960s. In his teens Povilas was conscripted into the Soviet army and sent to Russia, where he was given the option of military service or skating. He opted for skating and was teamed with Drobiazko. A very wise choice.

◀ Skate America | Colorado Springs | October 2000
Margarita and Povilas excel at expressing the character of the dance.

Born: December 21, 1971, Moscow; July 23, 1970, Kaunas

Hometowns: Moscow; Kaunas

Training Site: Moscow

Coach: Elena Tchaikovskaya

Choreographer: Elena Tchaikovskaya

RESULTS

1999: 6th Worlds
4th Grand Prix Finals
5th Europeans
3rd NHK

2000: 3rd Worlds
3rd Europeans
3rd Grand Prix Final
2nd Sparkassen Cup
2nd Skate America
2nd NHK

2001: 5th Worlds
4th Europeans
3rd Grand Prix Final

Worlds | Vancouver | March 2001

• When Lithuania became the first nation to gain independence from Russia, Povilas persuaded Margarita to represent Lithuania with him. They made their international debut in 1992.

They switched to coach Elena Tchaikovskaya in 1999 in order to improve their compulsory dances, which were holding them back.

Galit Chait & Sergei Sakhnovski

It took Galit Chait and Sergei Sakhnovski many years to become an overnight success.

Most of the skating community began to notice Israel's ice dancers only in 2000 when they defied custom by rocketing to fifth place at Worlds in Nice, France. They had been 13th the year before and a leap of eight places into the upper echelon is rare in ice dancing. Yet Chait and Sakhnovski weren't newcomers to the sport. They had languished in the middle ranks for years, together and with other partners, before their spectacular rise up the ladder in 2000.

In 1999 they changed from one world-class Russian coach to another, and that was the spark that ignited the couple. Their new coach was Tatiana Tarasova, best known for developing championship metal out of talented raw materials.

"She helped us have a new outlook on skating with new ideas, new choreography, new moves." Chait explains. "She tells us to do every move like it's the last time you're going to do it." But at the end of the 2001 season they switched to coach Natalia Dubova, to get more individual attention.

Chait, who was born in Israel but grew up in the U.S., and Sakhnovski, who started ice dancing at the age of eight in Moscow, made their world debut at Edmonton in 1996, finishing 23rd. After that it was 18th, 14th and 13th before they came into the 1999–2000 season with more speed, dramatic presentation and confidence.

Sakhnovski says the couple's motivation is, "to show the strength in our skating."

They already have.

Born: January 29, 1975, Kfar-Saba, Israel; May 15, 1975, Moscow

Hometown: Moscow

Training Site: Stamford, Connecticut

Coach: Natalia Dubova

Choreographer: Natalia Dubova

RESULTS

1998: 14th Olympics
14th Worlds
5th Trophee Lalique
5th NHK
5th Sparkassen Cup

1999: 13th Worlds
10th Europeans
5th NHK
6th Trophee Lalique

2000: 5th Worlds
6th Europeans
2nd Skate Canada
3rd Cup of Russia
4th Skate America
1st Skate Israel

2001: 6th Worlds
4th Grand Prix Final
5th Europeans

⬆ Skate Canada | Mississauga | November 2000

◀ Skate Canada | Mississauga | November 2000
Galit and Sergei have stunning speed and charisma and are great innovators and risk takers with their sensational moves.

• Galit and Sergei get a huge amount of fan mail. She keeps the letters and answers them all. "I remember when I was little and always looked up to the skaters, if somebody wouldn't sign something I was devastated," Galit explains. "I never want to do that to somebody. I think it's special."

Kati Winkler
& Rene Lohse

Although they both love ice dancing, Kati Winkler and Rene Lohse didn't choose figure skating. It chose them.

Winkler and Lohse grew up in the old nation of East Germany. When each of them was four years old, in kindergarten, Winkler and Lohse were identified as having athletic talent and were selected to be figure skaters.

They started in singles and had early successes, but neither was good at landing triple jumps. So, at 12, Lohse left skating and began playing soccer. Meanwhile, Winkler had back problems and had to stop singles skating in 1987. She was told she could switch to ice dancing, but there hadn't been any ice dance training in East Germany for 18 years. "I loved to skate and wanted to try it, but had no idea what to do," Winkler remembers. "So I started with some girls and we just had a 'book of rules.' There were no boys."

Winkler remembered Lohse, who was in her class at school until 1985, and asked him to become her dance partner. He said yes.

"I was surprised, but I was yearning to skate again after two years," he said.

Since there was no ice dance coach, the new couple was assigned to Knut Schubert, a Berlin pairs coach. Other skaters laughed at them and said dancing wasn't a sport.

"But their minds changed quickly when they saw us work out of nothing and win the national junior title, and go to two Junior World Championships," Lohse says.

The couple finished eighth at the 1992 World Juniors, but just as their career was blossoming, their country was united with West Germany. They had to work their way up through the ranks again. By 1996, Winkler and Lohse were German champions. That year, they moved from Berlin to Oberstdorf to work with coach Martin Skotnicky.

Like many German athletes, Winkler and Lohse have become members of the German army, which pays them a salary while they compete. The support paid off when they

were guaranteed an Olympic berth with their sixth-place finish at 2001 Worlds.

"Believe in yourself," Winkler says of the long, difficult road she and Lohse have traveled. "Have patience and live your dreams."

- In the army, Kati and Rene took basic training and attended seminars. Kati also finished vocational training at Mercedes-Benz and Rene went to university, all while skating.

> **Born:** January 16, 1974, Karl-Marx-Stadt;
> September 23, 1973, Berlin
>
> **Hometown:** Berlin
>
> **Training Site:** Oberstdorf
>
> **Coach:** Martin Skotnicky
>
> **Choreographers:** Marc Bongaerts,
> Martin Skotnicky, Werner Lipowsky

RESULTS

1999: 7th Worlds
6th Europeans
2nd Nation's Cup
4th Skate America

2000: 6th Worlds
5th Europeans
3rd NHK
3rd Trophee Lalique
4th Sparkassen Cup

2001: 6th Worlds
5th Grand Prix Final
5th Europeans

*Words | Nice
March 2000*

Worlds | Vancouver | March 2001

Kati and Rene can do lighthearted and serious equally well.

Elena Grushina & Ruslan Goncharov

Elena Grushina and Ruslan Goncharov would rather dance than jump. So it's a good thing they each decided to give up singles skating.

When Grushina started skating at the age of four, and Goncharov started at the age of six, neither chose ice dancing. Eventually Goncharov realized he would grow to be too tall (he's 6'1") to be an effective singles skater while Grushina came to see that skating in a couple would be more interesting than training on her own. Since each had studied ballet from a young age, ice dancing seemed an obvious destination.

They were in the same training group in their hometown of Odessa, Ukraine, but coaches there decided that Grushina should skate with Mikhail Tashliski and Goncharov should team up with Eleonora Grinsaya. But within two years both partnerships were over. It seemed natural that the two remaining partners should join forces—so natural that they became a couple away from the rink as well. They married in 1995.

Sometimes the hardest part of ice dancing is the waiting. Irina Romanova and Igor Yaroshenko were dominating Ukranian ice dancing, so it took time for Grushina and Goncharov to make their mark. Grushina and Goncharov made their world debut in 1994 and finished 18th. In the brief absence of Romanova and Yaroshenko, they won their first national title in 1995 but could not win another until 1999.

They hovered in the middle of the world ice dance pack for several years, climbing as high as 13th at 1998 Worlds. By then they had moved to Newark, Delaware, to train with Natalia Linichuk and Gennadi Karponosov, because their rink in Odessa closed down. They now consider Delaware home.

When Romanova and Yaroshenko retired after the 1998 Olympic season, allowing Grushina and Goncharov more international exposure, they pushed their way into the Worlds' top 10, where they've remained ever since.

"Our goal is to make it to the top in Worlds, of course," says Grushina, "and to fulfill ourselves as skaters."

Born: January 8, 1975, Odessa; January 20, 1973, Odessa

Hometown: Odessa

Training Site: Newark, Delaware

Coaches: Natalia Linichuk, Gennadi Karponosov

Choreographer: Natalia Linichuk

RESULTS

1999: 8th Worlds
7th Europeans
2nd Skate Canada
4th NHK

2000: 7th Worlds
8th Europeans
4th Skate Canada
4th NHK

2001: 8th Worlds
7th Europeans

- Elena's hobbies are reading and billiards. Ruslan prefers tennis and fishing.

Skate Canada | Mississauga November 2000

Skate Canada | Mississauga | November 2000
Wonderful facial expression and wonderful footwork characterize this team.

Naomi Lang & Peter Tchernyshev

Peter Tchernyshev insists that he feels "more like I am just a citizen of planet Earth than I am a Russian or an American." On January 29, 2001, at a ceremony in Detroit, Tchernyshev became an American citizen. At his side was Naomi Lang, with whom he had already won three consecutive American ice dancing championships.

Tchernyshev was born in Russia and followed a family tradition by enrolling in the Soviet skating system. He skated singles until he was 18, when injuries began impeding his jumps, so he concentrated on ice dancing. In 1992, he moved to the U.S., and at the 1996 U.S. Nationals he noticed a 15-year-old junior dancer who was "very expressive" and suggested they form a partnership. Naomi Lang agreed.

Lang was inspired to start skating as an eight-year-old after seeing the Ice Capades. Since lessons were expensive, her mother, Leslie Dixon, scrimped and saved, and she and her daughter sewed Naomi's costumes themselves at the kitchen table.

Naomi is a natural, passionate dancer, but because Tchernyshev is eight years older and was more experienced, at the beginning it was an imbalanced partnership. But gradually Lang matured, and early in 2001 Tchernyshev said, "she is doing some things better than me." They are blessed with attractive lines and enviable technique. When they moved to New Jersey in 2000 to work with former world champion Sasha Zhulin, he injected a spark of fresh enthusiasm into their work.

- Naomi is a member of the west coast Native American tribe, the Karuk, and wants to be a role model for Native American children.

Born: December, 18, 1978, Arcata, California; February 6, 1971, St. Petersburg, Russia

Hometown: Allegan, Michigan; Waterford, Michigan

Training Site: Hackensack, New Jersey

Coach: Alexander Zhulin

Choreographer: Alexander Zhulin

RESULTS

1998: 5th Skate America

1999: 10th Worlds
3rd Four Continents
3rd Skate America
5th Trophee Lalique

2000: 8th Worlds
1st Four Continents
1st U.S. Nationals
5th Skate America
4th Trophee Lalique

2001: 9th Worlds
2nd Four Continents

Four Continents Salt Lake City | February 2001
Naomi and Peter are classical and pure in their lines.

Four Continents | Salt Lake City February 2001   Four Continents | Salt Lake City February 2001

Marie-France Dubreuil & Patrice Lauzon

Marie-France Dubreuil and Patrice Lauzon had fallen in love but they were the last to know.

"Everybody saw it except us; it took us some time to recognize it," Dubreuil recalls with a smile. "But you can only fight your feelings for awhile."

The couple stopped fighting their feelings a year after they became an ice-dancing team in 1995. Even that partnership took them some time to figure out. They had been good friends and had trained at the same Montreal rink for years, with different partners. Dubreuil won a Junior World bronze medal with Bruno Yvars and also skated with Thomas Morbacher, while Lauzon was fourth at World Juniors with Chantal Lefebvre.

"We were all at Patrice's cottage, just friends having fun," Dubreuil said. "Patrice was taking a year off and I had quit my partnership. I said, 'Maybe we should try, because we get along fine and it would be fun.' And it worked."

Right away. They finished a surprising fourth in their first Nationals. But then they hit a plateau, stalling in fourth place for three more years. The last time, in 1999, they had a bronze locked up until a freak fall seconds from the end of their program. They became discouraged, and considered retiring, but decided to give it one more year.

And what a year it was. With Shae-Lynn Bourne and Victor Kraatz sidelined by injury, Dubreuil and Lauzon won the Canadian championship in January 2000, then took a silver medal at Four Continents. Impressed by their combination of North American and European styles (they spend three weeks each year training in Lyon, France) judges placed them 10th in their impressive world championship debut.

With the return of Bourne and Kraatz and the top-10

Born: August 11, 1974, Montreal;
November 26, 1975, Montreal

Hometown: Boisbriand, Quebec

Training Site: Boucherville, Quebec

Coaches: Sylvie Fullum, Francois Vallee

Choreographer: Murielle Boucher-Zazoui

RESULTS

1999: 4th Skate Canada

2000: 10th Worlds
2nd Four Continents
3rd Skate Canada
1st Canadian Nationals

2001: 11th Worlds
6th Grand Prix Final
3rd Four Continents
2nd Canadian Nationals

- Patrice started figure skating at nine, to improve his hockey skills. He played both sports until he was 14. Marie-France's mother didn't want her to start skating, so the resourceful girl asked her grandmother to buy her skates for her fifth birthday.

Bulgarians, Dubreuil and Lauzon slipped to 11th in 2001, but they were satisifed. Dubreuil said "It's a little personal victory for us."

Worlds | Vancouver
March 2001

Worlds | Vancouver
March 2001

Worlds | Vancouver | March 2001

Intensity and passion make Marie-France and Patrice a team to reckon with.

Isabelle Delobel & Olivier Schoenfelder

sabelle Delobel and Olivier Schoenfelder met during training course in the French ice dance capital of Lyon when they were just 12 years old.

It was 1990, a time of excitement and unlimited promise for the sport in their country. Isabelle and Paul Duchesnay had just won their second world medal, France's first podium placings in ice dance since 1962. Several other young French couples were on the rise. And the nucleus was Lyon, where the training course was being supervised by Russians Irina Moiseeva and Andrei Minenkov, the legendary "Min and Mo," one of the greatest dance teams in history.

Delobel and Schoenfelder had come to the camp with different partners, but Min and Mo liked the combination of a tall blond and the shorter brunette, and put them together. They've been together ever since. Delobel moved to Lyon from nearby Clermont-Ferrand, and Schoenfelder left his hometown of Belfort, near the Swiss border, so they could train with renowned dance teacher Lydie Bontems at the Lyon Ice Dance Centre.

With their classic, but dynamic, style Delobel and Schoenfelder were chosen to represent France internationally, winning silver at World Juniors in 1996.

After spending time in the U.S. with Tatiana Tarasova in 1999, they returned to Lyon to train under Muriel Boucher-Zazoui, with 2000 world champions Marina Anissina and Gwendal Peizerat.

In 2000 Delobel and Schoenfelder reached the podium at a Grand Prix event for the first time, winning bronze at Skate Canada, and had their best Worlds, finishing 11th. But they're aiming much higher.

"We are finding our own style," said Delobel, "so in the next couple of years we can reach the top five."

- Isabelle and Olivier liked their 2001 freeskate to Johnny Hallyday music so much, they're keeping it for exhibitions.

Born: June 17, 1978, Clermont-Ferrand; November 30, 1977, Belfort

Hometown: Lyon

Training Site: Lyon

Coach: Muriel Boucher-Zazoui

Choreographers: Nikolai Morozov, Tatiana Tarasova

Worlds | Vancouver | March 2001
This team has a commanding presence.

RESULTS

1999: 14th Worlds
12th Europeans
3rd Skate Canada
7th Trophee Lalique

2000: 11th Worlds
9th Europeans
5th Sparkassen Cup
5th Trophee Lalique

2001: 13th Worlds
10th Europeans

Worlds | Nice | March 2000

Albena Denkova & Maxim Staviyski

If it weren't for bad luck, they would have had no luck at all.

Albena Denkova and Maxim Staviyski made a triumphant return to the world championships in 2001, with Bulgaria's first top 10 finish in ice dancing. That followed one of the most ill-fated years to ever befall a dance team.

In 2000, the couple had to withdraw from Europeans because Staviyski came down with a heavy case of pneumonia for three weeks. Then, when the couple was headed for a top 10 placing at Worlds, Denkova collided with U.S. dancer Peter Tchernyshev, at a practice on the morning of the freedance. His blade severed two tendons and a muscle in her lower leg. It was gruesome scene. When she finally began skating again, after many months, the leg ballooned horribly. But she persevered and the couple finished eighth at 2001 Europeans and 10th at Worlds.

Denkova began her athletic career as an artistic gymnast, moved to skating when she was nine—"but I could not jump"—and took up ice dancing when she was 12.

Meanwhile, Staviyski was growing up in Russia as a singles skater. But when he was 12 he broke his leg and his jumping power diminished. He became an ice dancer.

Staviyski moved to Bulgaria and formed an innovative, creative team with Denkova. They train part of the year with coach Alexei Gorshkov near Moscow, then return to Sofia where they work mostly alone.

Alone, but not unknown. Their success, and their courage, have made figure skating what Denkova calls, "the most famous winter sport in our country."

🔺 Skate Canada | Kamloops | November 1998
Albena and Maxim's creative programs are a feast for the eye.

Born: December 3, 1974, Sofia; November 16, 1977, Rostov-na-Don

Hometown: Sofia

Training Sites: Moscow and Sofia

Coach: Alexei Gorshkov

Choreographer: Sergei Petukhov

RESULTS

1999: 11th Worlds
9th Europeans
6th NHK
3rd Sparkassen Cup

2000: 1st Finlandia Trophy

2001: 8th Europeans
10th Worlds

- Albena has a university degree in economics, but may become a clothing designer. Maxim has a degree from a sports institute and may go into coaching in Bulgaria, where skating has become more popular.

Skate Canada | Kamloops | November 1998

Tanith Belbin & Benjamin Agosto

What goes around comes around, but not necessarily in the same form.

In March of 2001, Tanith Belbin returned to Vancouver's GM Place, four years after she'd first competed in the massive arena. At the 1997 Canadian Championships, Belbin was a 12-year-old pairs skater living in a Montreal suburb. She and partner Benjamin Barrucco won a silver medal in novice pairs.

At the 2001 World Championships, Belbin was a 16-year-old ice dancer, living in a Detroit suburb and skating for the U.S. She and another Benjamin—19-year-old Benjamin Agosto—finished a commendable 17th in their world debut.

"I spent a year in Canada looking for an ice dancing partner, but couldn't find one," Belbin says of her cross-border alliance.

Agosto's coaches Igor Shpilband and Elizabeth Coates ran into Belbin's coach, Paul Wirtz, at the Nagano Olympics. As a result, Belbin moved to Agosto's training base in Detroit, and the international alliance was forged.

"It's something you see very often in ice dancing," Agosto said. "You have to look everywhere for the best partner and I'm just thankful for this."

Belbin and her mother Michelle, a skating coach and costume designer, moved to Michigan in 1998. A year later, her father Charles obtained a transfer, so he and son Lucas could join the rest of the family.

"It was a great sacrifice for everyone," Belbin says. "It shows what kind of support we have."

The new couple enjoyed quick success, winning the Junior Grand Prix Final in 2001. Belbin and Agosto are permitted to compete at Worlds, but in order to represent the U.S. at the Olympics, Belbin must become an American citizen; it's a process that cannot be completed in time for the 2002 Games.

"It's out of the question. We knew that going in to the partnership" Belbin says. "But it was something we were willing to give up for the long-term sake of our partnership."

Born: July 11, 1984, Kingston, Ontario; January 15, 1982, Chicago

Hometowns: Montreal; Chicago

Training Site: Bloomfield Hills, Michigan

Coaches: Igor Shpilband, Elizabeth Coates

Choreographer: Igor Shpilband

RESULTS

2000: 1st U.S. Junior Nationals

2001: 17th Worlds
1st Junior Grand Prix Final
2nd U.S. Nationals

• Tanith and Benjamin were still juniors when they competed at 2001 Worlds.

Worlds | Vancouver | March 2001